To: Bill Chorske

Thanks for being my friend and ...nter. Your
advice, given in "ve ... most appreciated
and reflecting ...

SERIAL ENTREPRENEUR

Balancing Business and Family to
Achieve True Wealth and Happiness

With Life Lessons Learned

Jack D. Gulati

Reading Eagle Press
340 Court Street
Reading, PA 19601

First Reading Eagle Press hardcover edition September 2012

READING EAGLE PRESS and colophon are registered trademarks
of Reading Eagle Company.

For information about special discounts for bulk purchases, guest appearances, and book
signings, please contact Jack D. Gulati at jdg@jackgulati.com

Designed by Jacqueline Schmehl

Manufactured in the United States of America
1 3 5 7 9 10 8 6 4 2
Library of Congress Control Number: 2012915843.

ISBN 978-0-9882741-0-5 (Hard Cover)
ISBN 978-0-9882741-1-2 (Soft Cover)
ISBN 978-0-9882741-2-9 (ebook)

Table of Contents

CONTENTS

CONTENTS

For Rosemary,

J. David II, Charles, Michael,

their spouses Loretta, Jennifer, and Allison;

My Grandchildren

and

My Parents,

Jagjit Lal Gulati and Leela Wanti Sethi Gulati,

whom I miss dearly and to whom I owe much.

Acknowledgments

Many people had a hand in helping me translate my idea to write an autobiography into a finished book. First and foremost, I would like to thank my bride of thirty-nine years, Rosemary, a lifelong partner who jogged my memory about many events, read every draft, and wielded her editorial pencil with exceptional skill. My sister, Purnima, was also especially helpful in recalling details of our childhood in India and our years in New York City. My three sons reviewed those sections of the book that describe their youth and professional careers, making sure I got the details right. Also, I am deeply indebted to Larry Mazzeno who spent a year helping me write this book, in particular, researching background information and walking me through the process of getting the book published. My appreciation also goes to Terry Scott Reed who helped edit the manuscript.

In addition I want to acknowledge the many professional associates who have helped in making me a successful entrepreneur, and who have taught me many valuable lessons about business and life. These include my colleagues at Fidelity Technologies, Telectronic, TeleAlarm, SafetyCare, Stokesay Castle, Transrex, and other firms with which I have been involved over the years. Special thanks goes to my Board of Advisors who offered sound advice that helped me grow personally, guided me in businesses, and helped me to avoid many pitfalls: Attorney General Edwin Meese III, General John W. Vessey, Jr., Claude Romy, Joseph P. Freeman, William Chorske, John C. Beck M.D., Stanley Kabala, Daniel Luthringhauser, and Karl Bornschein.

Again I want to acknowledge my sons, this time as professional colleagues who have taken the businesses I have built and made them even more successful. If I have any regret, it is that my parents did not live to see my accomplishments. I believe they would have been proud. I know I owe much to them for having taught me the value of hard work and vision, and for instilling in me the desire to be my own boss. I hope my career serves as a fitting tribute to their love and guidance. I believe they still look over me and provide guidance when I fail.

Foreword

For decades America's book stores have been filled with "how to" books, including many on "management", "family relations", and "effective personal habits." It is rare to find a book that combines all of these themes with a fascinating personal story of integrity, perseverance, and success. Readers of *Serial Entrepreneur: Balancing Business and Family to Achieve True Wealth and Happiness* will find valuable lessons for "the business of life." The author, Jack D. Gulati, has provided in this book a record of achievement and forthright commentary that make him an ideal mentor for aspiring entrepreneurs and others seeking accomplishment in their lives.

I first met Jack Gulati when I was serving as U.S. Attorney General in the Reagan Administration. Jack participated in the 1986 White House Conference on Small Business and later served as a member of the Small Business Advisory Committee of the Federal Communications Commission. I don't think that either of us realized at the time that we would become involved in one of Jack's business ventures. However, after I left government service and took a position at The Heritage Foundation, our paths crossed again at a political event in Wayne, Pennsylvania. Jack was forming an advisory board for Fidelity Technologies and asked if I would like to become a member. He did not ask me to invest, nor did he offer compensation. My task would be to provide advice and help him recruit other members to the board. I was intrigued by the proposition and agreed. I never regretted the decision.

Under Jack Gulati's leadership, Fidelity Technologies grew from a start-up that initially struggled to get business into one of the country's most dynamic suppliers of parts and equipment for the Department of Defense. Over the years I served on the Fidelity Technologies board, I came to know Jack quite well and realized that he is a born "entrepreneur." I suspect that not a day goes by that he isn't looking for the next opportunity to invest his time, talent, and treasure to help bring another new idea into the commercial marketplace. But what is particularly impressive about Jack is his integrity, his generous treatment of other people, and his commitment to the wellbeing of those around him.

In Serial Entrepreneur Jack Gulati explains what motivates him and how he has managed to keep his zeal for entrepreneurial ventures alive for more than four decades. He also tells some engaging family stories that round out the portrait of a man intensely committed to his business enterprises and to his family. You won't find a lot of business-school platitudes in this book. Instead, you'll get solid advice from a highly successful entrepreneur who has had his share of ups and downs over his remarkable career. What strikes me, and what I am sure will strike other readers, is the remarkable honesty of the narrative. Jack isn't hesitant to admit his failures, and he takes the time to point out the lessons he's learned from them. That is why there is a ring of authenticity to the accounts of his successes, and a sense that the lessons he offers about things he did right are going to be of value to those who choose to follow his advice.

Those of us born and raised in the United States sometimes take for granted the opportunities available to us, not realizing the unique opportunity we all have to realize what people from all around the world describe as "The American Dream." Coming from India as a teen, Jack Gulati managed to realize that dream by applying the skills he learned on the job and by remaining true to the values instilled in him by loving parents. His story demonstrates that America remains a country where freedom, opportunity, and the prospects for prosperity continue to remain available to those who seek them.

Edwin Meese III

Why a Serial Entrepreneur?

Why did I become a serial entrepreneur? Many people wish to become their own bosses and launch companies that they can grow and pass on to the next generation. Some entrepreneurs are happy and successful in creating a single company. Others may try and fail, but find success in their second or third company, and remain in that business for the rest of their working lives.

In my case, however, I have chosen to become involved in many companies—forty, to be precise. I had my share of

Bust of Jack presented by the employees of Stokesay Castle in 2011. *(Sculpture by Angelo Di Maria)*

failures, especially early in my career, as I was learning how to organize and finance start-up operations. I have also had the disappointing experience of buying into existing businesses that did not succeed, and the even more frustrating circumstance of experiencing success in turning around a moribund company, only to be dismissed by other stockholders. Yet when I had finally established Fidelity Technologies, and the business was turning a profit, I found myself looking around for other opportunities—some that would expand my current operations at Fidelity Technologies, and others that would provide me with new challenges and get me out of my comfort zone.

I believe that my zeal for launching new ventures, even while existing ones are doing well, illustrates something about my character and may reveal one of the important attributes of a serial entrepreneur. I have found that I am most happy when I am involved in doing something I've never tried before. I love learning about new industries and new technologies. I am exhilarated by the process of negotiating a purchase or sale, or reorganizing a company to serve new markets. I love long-range planning, and setting out strategies for a business to rise to a place of prominence in its industry. At the same time, I realize that I am not content with the day-to-day management of companies—even ones that are recognized as industry leaders. I do not like focusing on routine operational matters, even though I recognize that a company's success depends on executing daily tasks efficiently and effectively. My success comes from launching new ventures and then hiring good people to manage operations, while I look for opportunities to expand my business portfolio and my personal horizons.

Why I Wrote This Book and How Readers May Benefit from It

Building a successful enterprise while also fostering strong family ties presents unique challenges. The entrepreneur cannot measure success by financial gains alone, but must consider personal satisfaction and a well-balanced family life as well. This book attempts to address those issues.

SERIAL ENTREPRENEUR: Balancing Business and Family to Achieve True Wealth and Happiness is a book for all entrepreneurs—both waiting-to-be entrepreneurs contemplating the idea of striking out on their own and those already involved in running their own businesses. If you are considering the possibility of launching your own company, I offer encouragement; if you have vision and the willingness to work hard at something about which you are passionate, you too can succeed as an entrepreneur. If you have recently become an entrepreneur, this guide will help you draft a blueprint for your own career and show you what you can do to reach your goals while avoiding some of the pitfalls I encountered as I moved from one business to another. For the well-established entrepreneur, I offer practical advice about solidifying your business gains and creating a workable succession plan to enable you to pass your business on to your heirs. Then the next generation can continue to build on the foundation you have laid for them. As an alternative, I will show you how to exit your business via sale, merger or some other way that allows the business to continue operating.

In this book I address some of the important questions every entrepreneur must answer: How do you become an entrepreneur? What do you do with your business? When do you acknowledge that a business is beyond your capability? When do you recognize that it is time to turn over the business to the next generation? Should you sell? Liquidate? Merge? How do you transition to a new generation of managers?

This is not a textbook. Instead, this narrative is my philosophy for entrepreneurial success. I believe that, while success cannot be guaranteed, you can put yourself in a better position to succeed by learning from others what it takes to be an entrepreneur. As you read my story, you will see illustrations of attributes that most entrepreneurs possess and some examples where the failure to exhibit those qualities cost me dearly.

My wife, Rosemary, often tells people that two of my distinguishing characteristics are the ability to make things happen and the perseverance to get others to join in my vision— to make them believe that they, too, can succeed. While she may be right, these attributes flow from the most important quality an entrepreneur must possess: the ability to envision the future in which he or she will be successful and realize lifelong objectives. The vision must have the staying power to withstand the ups and downs of a volatile economy, coupled with an exit strategy that will allow the business to be passed on to the next generation or sold to provide a financial legacy. Having a vision, then, is the first step toward success as an entrepreneur. As long as I can remember, I envisioned that I would create businesses that I could pass on to my children. My education and willingness to work hard would be the means of achieving these goals.

Constantly preparing to take advantage of opportunity is another important attribute. Often one hears about an entrepreneur "being lucky." While I would not deny that some opportunities seem to arise from nowhere, I have always subscribed to the observation of the first-century Roman philosopher, Seneca: "Luck is what happens when preparation meets opportunity." Working on projects throughout your life and constantly exploring new avenues for using your business talents will prepare you to take advantage of the opportunities that come your way.

A critically important quality is the willingness to take risks. Too often, entrepreneurs fail to succeed because they are unwilling to risk failure. Certainly my story is not one of uninterrupted successes, and in this book I try to be as honest about my failures as I am about my successes. I want readers to realize that it is possible to suffer setbacks and still reach the goals they set for themselves. Those thinking about becoming entrepreneurs, or already engaged in entrepreneurial activity, must realize that it is highly likely that at some point they will fail.

Throughout this account of my career, I stop on occasion to point out lessons I have learned from my experiences. You will see that they are very basic and fundamental. They are purposely stated that way so that they do not appear to be "lectures," and this book does not turn into a textbook.

Businessman Robert Kiyosaki, author of the popular *Rich Dad* series of books, points out that the test of a true entrepreneur comes when the first venture fails. Those who are not serious about making a go of things on their own will simply retreat to a safer environment, perhaps working for someone else. I certainly felt those sentiments at times. Having already been successful working for others, I was confident that, at any time, I could have gone back to a salaried position and built a comfortable life for my family. However, any success that I achieved working for others would be hollow compared to the feeling of creating my own business.

Truly great entrepreneurs use failures as lessons to improve their chances for future success by revisiting their plans, or creating new visions based on their experiences. The first business failure, or any future one, should not indicate that you have failed; rather, the time and effort and resources you have put into these ventures should be considered an investment in yourself, as the experiences will prepare you for the eventual success you will enjoy if you continue to pursue your vision diligently. Take the case of Henry Ford, for example. For years Ford worked for someone else while he saved money, and spent his evenings and weekends trying to build a better version of that new-fangled contraption, the horseless carriage. By 1896 he had built a prototype, and he immediately sought financing to establish his own automobile manufacturing business. To great expectations, Ford opened the doors to his new factory in 1899. Eighteen months later, the company closed down. Undaunted, Ford continued experimenting, and in 1903, with the backing of a number of other Detroit businessmen, he launched the Ford Motor Company, and went on during his lifetime to create one of the most successful companies in America. He became one of the richest men in America.

We cannot all be Henry Fords, but I believe all of us have the potential to build a business for ourselves. Some businesses will make millions, while others will earn only thousands; however, they can all bring great personal satisfaction if you possess the ingenuity, tenacity, and integrity to make it through tough times, and create an enterprise that will generate income and become a legacy for your family.

This is not the first book by a successful entrepreneur that offers advice by sharing personal successes and failures, and points out lessons that can help readers chart a course to financial and personal success. Quite a few books have been written by business executives such as Warren Buffett, Donald Trump, or Jack Welsh, who have managed large private or public companies. Numerous books have been written by academics that lay out business theory, occasionally citing cases that support their approach to business management and development. I offer something a bit different. I share first-hand experiences in running small to modest-size companies—the backbone of American enterprise in the twenty-first century. One distinguishing characteristic of this book is the emphasis I place on the importance of family, and the need for an entrepreneur to balance business affairs with family activities. Many successful executives, both those who are in business for themselves and those who run large public or private companies, end up achieving their financial goals at the expense of family life, a sad situation, and one that does not have to occur. I believe entrepreneurs do not have to choose between family and career. In fact, I think one cannot be truly happy and truly successful unless family obligations are satisfied, and family is made the centerpiece of one's life. Throughout this book I give examples of ways one can make conscious efforts to include the family in one's business activities and prepare them to take over the business, should they wish to do so, when it comes time for the founder to step aside.

I hope you will let me show you how you, too, can become an entrepreneur, achieving success in business as well as in family life. The rewards can go far beyond the accumulation of material wealth.

PART I

Growing Up

My story begins in India. In 1942, India boasted a population of about 400 million people, three times that of the United States. The world was at war, and thousands of Indians were serving in the armed forces, many stationed far from home. Called up to fight on behalf of the British Empire in support of the Allies in their war against Hitler and the Axis nations, they were destined for places like North Africa and Italy, where they would distinguish themselves in combat. At that time, India was a British colony, ruled by a colonial governor. The British had come to India as traders in the seventeenth century. By the nineteenth century they had made the Indian subcontinent part of the far-flung British Empire, and Indians were relegated to second-class citizenship in their own homeland. Though the Indian population acquiesced to British rule, calls for independence had been raised almost as soon as the British established "the Raj," their system of colonial governance.

By the 1920s, however, a movement for Indian independence

was well organized. Led by men like Mohandas Gandhi, who would become known throughout the world as Mahatma Gandhi, the idea that India should once again be self-governing was beginning to gain momentum. It became the subject of serious negotiation between emissaries of the British Crown and Indian leaders in the 1940s, as the Empire was struggling to fight a global war and maintain control over its increasingly unruly subjugate nations. At the same time, an internal struggle was taking place among factions inside India to determine the future of the country once the British left. Gandhi and his supporters envisioned a unified India under democratic rule. However, a vocal group of Muslims, led by Mohammed Ali Jinnah, were making increasingly stronger claims that the country should be divided so that Muslims, which made up a significant minority inside India, could establish their own majority Muslim state.

Amid this growing political turmoil I was born in Gujranwala in the northwest province of Punjab. In the official 1901 census the city had a population of thirty thousand, but by 1942 it was on its way to becoming the industrial metropolis that would be home to more than two million residents today. I came into the world on September 20, 1942—or so my mother told me. No birth records were kept in India at the time, and most babies were born at home, where mothers were assisted by family members and "elder ladies" who came to aid with delivery. I was given the name Ashok Kumar Gulati, which I retained until I moved to America and applied for citizenship. These were names of great tradition and promise. "Ashok" means "without sorrow," suggesting that my parents expected me to be a happy child; the name also recalls the great third-century B.C. Indian emperor Ashoka. "Kumar" derives from the Sanskrit word for "prince." In keeping with Indian custom, my family commissioned an astrologer to create a horoscope that would chart my future. This elaborate document has some interesting predictions. I have reproduced the first page and included a translation of the entire document in Appendix A.

I was a middle child: my sister Kamlesh Kamari (now Purnima or Pat) Gulati (later Thomsen) was born nearly two years earlier on January 1, 1941, and my brother Davinder Pal Gulati arrived three years after me on March 15, 1945.

My mother, Leela Wanti Sethi, was likewise born in Gujranwala in the Punjab region of India, on January 31, 1920. Her father was a well-to-do merchant who traded in food commodities (rice, beans, wheat) at his store in Gujranwala. She was the youngest of four daughters and had an older and a younger brother. She was pampered by her parents and was close to her sisters and her many cousins. She was better educated than most women of her time and was enrolled in a course that would lead to a medical degree. However, when she was nineteen years of age, my grandfather arranged a marriage for her with the son of another affluent merchant who had originally lived in the area but had moved to Delhi for business reasons.

My father, Jagjit Lal Gulati, was a native of the Punjab region as well, born in the village of Multan on January 1, 1915. He had four older brothers and two sisters. His father was also a wealthy merchant and a member of the Arora caste, a mercantile community concentrated in the Punjab. One economic historian has described the Aroras as having controlled much of India's commerce with central Asia, Afghanistan, and Tibet. They were the dominant merchant class in the region where my father's family lived, and were known for being industrious and willing to engage in every kind of enterprise where money was to be made. During the late nineteenth and early twentieth century the Aroras became important landowners in the regions where they resided.

My paternal grandfather always planned to bring his sons into his businesses, as was the custom in India in those days. At the time, and still today, families had the expectation that a son would take over a family business; there was no buying and selling of businesses as is common in the United States. Of course, when there were several sons in a family, it was sometimes necessary for one or more of them to go into another business or profession. My father's eldest brother went to medical school; the others became businessmen. My father was well educated. He had passed the National Matriculation Examination and had begun university studies, but he left school to help his father with one of his businesses. My father and a brother became proprietors of my grandfather's chain of liquor stores, some of which were located in posh sections of Delhi. Once my father and his brothers were established in the family's businesses, my grandparents retired, and their sons supported them—another Indian custom.

When my parents married in 1939, my mother became the first in her family to move away from Gujranwala. She went with my father to Delhi and joined his family's household. Such was the custom of the day; wives of sons became like daughters to their mothers-in-laws, and helped with household chores. However, my paternal grandparents had three other sons and a daughter, thus their home eventually became too small to accommodate the extended family. My father then bought his own home at #13 Hanuman Road in an upscale neighborhood in Delhi.

I was born in Gujranwala rather than Delhi because my mother's family remained there. At the time it was common practice in India for expectant mothers to return to their mother's homes to give birth. The familiar surroundings and the presence of family members gave new mothers a support network during those first few months. Several months after I was born, my mother brought me back to Delhi to be with my father and sister.

Our family had more resources than many people in India, but we were not as well off as the upper middle class. There were servants in the home to handle most of the routine chores. We attended school in the morning, and had tutors at home in the afternoon to supplement our education. I was a precocious and outspoken student even at an early age. At a later date my mother reminded me that when I was very little, certainly no more than six, I told my tutor, "You can't teach me anything. I learned all I need to know in my mother's womb!"

The family home was a single-story dwelling with a flat roof. My sister, brother, and I studied up on the roof sitting cross-legged. We covered our heads in turbans, wound in the Hindu style so as to create a cloth tail covering the neck to keep off hot breezes. On the same roof, just about twenty feet from where we usually sat, was a coffee roaster that my grandfather used to roast coffee beans for sale. Unbeknownst to us at the time, the chemicals leeching from the beans had, over the years, gradually eroded the structure of the roof. One day while we were studying quietly, the roof gave way. We and the coffee machine plunged down into the main house some twenty feet below! Miraculously, no one was hurt. Looking back, I can see how lucky I was—or how a Providential Hand was protecting me.

Turmoil after World War II

It is not my intention to write a history book, but at this point I think it is important for me to expand my focus to include something about the state of affairs in India, to help explain what happened to my family when I was a small child, and how these events affected my future. Throughout the Second World War British officials negotiated with Indian leaders to develop a plan to grant the country independence. There were many proposals made and rejected, but not much progress occurred until the conclusion of the war. In 1945 Great Britain was in financial distress, and the British government decided it was time to grant their colonies independence as soon as possible, to avoid the heavy costs of maintaining an imperial presence in places thousands of miles away. Sadly, by this time the independence movement in India had become factionalized, largely along religious lines. The population was approximately 70 percent Hindu. Muslims were a large but distinct minority, with Sikhs a smaller but vocal sect. Gandhi and his Congress Party had long advocated for a single nation in which religious liberties would be protected for all. But religious differences ran strong, and for nearly four decades the Muslim League had advocated for its own country where Muslims would make up the majority of the population.

Perhaps because the British were in a hurry to get out—or perhaps because of the intransigence of Muslim leaders like Jinnah who refused to negotiate with either the British or other Indian political groups unless they accepted the two-state solution—in early 1947 an agreement was reached to carve up India to create two nations. The coastal provinces and central sections of the country, where the majority of the people were Hindus, would become the independent Republic of India. The provinces in the northwest and northeast, where Muslims made up the majority, would become the Islamic Republic of Pakistan. Some of the provinces bordering Pakistan would be divided, with some areas remaining in India while others would become part of the new Muslim country.

Unfortunately, the Punjab was one such province. The region around Gujranwala was designated as part of Pakistan. My mother's family suddenly found themselves part of the Hindu minority, whose presence in the area was not welcome. They were certainly not alone in feeling unwanted. After the partition of India, they were forced to relocate. Throughout territories in the northwest and northeast, Hindus and Muslims began a mass exodus from communities where they were minorities, traveling to areas where they might feel safer among those who shared the same religious traditions. This migration was so great that the new Indian capital, the city of Delhi, now expanded and renamed New Delhi, became inundated with refugees who evacuated from regions that were now part of Pakistan. So many people from the Gujranwala region moved to the city that an entire section of New Delhi was called the Gujranwala Section. My mother's family joined the exodus, traveling by train, carriage, or on foot. The Indian rail system, never known for its speed or efficiency, was in particularly poor shape after the Second World War. The British had taken over many of the country's repair depots and turned them into factories to produce materials for the war, and virtually nothing was done to maintain the trains or rail lines during the six years the Empire was engaged in conflict. The trains were always overcrowded, and seeing people riding on the roofs of cars or hanging off the sides was not uncommon. The overcrowding of the trains during the migration was even worse. In addition, the countryside was wracked with violence during the months following the establishment of India and Pakistan. Sikhs and Hindus fled the northwest and far eastern provinces that were part of the new Pakistan; Muslims departed from the southern and central provinces that were part of the new India. When it was all over, nearly ten million people had migrated to new homes. Worse, sectarian violence claimed the lives of as many as a million people of all faiths. In the fall of 1947, when my mother's family was traveling, many trains filled with refugees were stopped, passengers told to disembark, and executions carried out. Hindus, Sikhs, and Muslims were all perpetrators and victims in this senseless bloodbath.

By luck or providence, our relatives arrived in Delhi unharmed, but they had lost everything they owned when they left Gujranwala. However, like my father, my mother's brother, Banarsi Dass Sethi, was an entrepreneur, so pulling up stakes and relocating proved only a temporary setback. Within a few months he established himself as a merchant, selling food and other similar commodities. He, his wife, and six children moved into our home, which was large enough to accommodate everyone. The Sethi family remained with us for years. While my father was away, my uncle, whom we called Mama Ji, meaning revered uncle, became the de facto head of our household and was our "father figure."

Jack (left) visiting with aunt, Santosh Sethi (Mata Ji), and uncle, Banarsi Dass Sethi (Mama Ji), in 1988 in Gujranwala Town, New Delhi.

Within a few months after our relatives resettled in New Delhi, Gandhi was assassinated. On January 30, 1948 an assassin approached him in a large crowd and shot him several times. He died a short time later. The assassin, a Hindu extremist, believed that Gandhi was responsible for the 1947 partition of India and the creation of Pakistan. Gandhi's funeral was held the following day. A great pyre was built overnight on the banks of the Jumna River that flowed through the city. I was one of the millions who turned out for Gandhi's funeral. Indian funerals were public events; the body was burned on a ceremonial pyre and the flame kept alive for days as mourners came by to toss flammable substances on the pyre, pray, and offer condolences. Even at my young age I knew Gandhi had been a great man and would probably become a god among Hindus, who believe that people become deities by doing good works. That sentiment was shared across the country, and people began speaking of him in these terms almost immediately, even though the Congress Party lobbied against his deification, preferring to have him recognized merely as a great soul (Mahatma). Personally, even though I was not yet six years old, the incident left a serious impression on me. Here was a leader who could free his people but not achieve the unity he sought for so long. It did not make sense.

Life in New Delhi, 1947-1958

As far back as I can remember my father had been an entrepreneur. He and my uncle were successful in operating their liquor stores until 1947, when India was partitioned. Unfortunately, when the Congress Party came to power, one of the first laws they passed forbade Indians from buying liquor. The government revoked my father's liquor license without compensation, so he suddenly found himself out of business. Unfortunately, the authorities did not cancel his debts to creditors, so he had to find a way to support his family and pay off those to whom he owed money. He managed to secure a job with a textile company, but the work took him overseas. I recall him working in the import/export business, mainly with textiles. He was affiliated with a company called Allied Textiles located in Bangkok; his principal commodity was silk. Later, when we moved to the United States, he imported ivory from India. While he was away, my mother stayed at home, as most Indian women did. She was the glue that held our family together.

Though he may not have been with the family very often, my father was a dedicated husband and very conscientious about providing for his family. My father's business took him all over the world, and travel in those days was tedious and time-consuming. Just getting from our home in New Delhi to the ports from which he had to sail was not an easy task. Most Indians traveled by train within the country, often on slow "locals" that sometimes averaged only fifteen miles per hour and made many stops between major cities. As a consequence, the 700-mile trip from New Delhi to the port at Bombay (now Mumbai) could take days. The 1,200 mile trip to Calcutta (Kolkata) took even longer.

International travel was no better. Before and immediately after the War, travel outside India was undertaken principally by ship because the fledgling airlines—Tata Airlines before the partition of India in 1947, Indian Airlines thereafter—did not initiate international service until the 1950s, and then only to London. My father had to make the 3,100 mile trip to Hong Kong by sea. A trip to New York required a three-week voyage to England, and then an additional ten to twelve days to New York City. He must have been delighted when, in 1956, he was able to fly to New York aboard Pan Am from London! My father's business took him to Thailand, Japan, and other countries in the Far East, as well as Europe and America. Over the course of a five-year period he accumulated passport entry stamps from the United States, the United Kingdom, France, Italy, Egypt, Iraq, Palestine, Burma, Thailand, China, Singapore, Malaysia, Hong Kong, and the Philippines.

There is no doubt that we all missed him when he was away. Looking back, it is not surprising to me that he was able to return home only once every twelve to eighteen months. My siblings and I were always happy to see our father when he came home, in part because he always brought toys and other treats for us children, and for my cousins as well, and even small presents for the servants. Once, I recall that we were all extremely disappointed when we learned that he had carried home nearly three dozen toys only to have them confiscated by Customs. The Nehru government, following Gandhi's teachings that India should become self-sufficient, was making it very difficult for foreign goods to enter the country. Nehru and his ministers felt that Indians should buy Indian goods only, not import items from abroad. Our disappointment probably did not match that of my mother, however, when the authorities also impounded a set of fine china for twenty-four that my father had to send back to Japan.

While he was away, my father stayed in touch regularly—no small feat in those days. Communication was not easy. There was no instantaneous contact through the internet; phone service was poor or, in some cases, nonexistent. In addition, international calls were prohibitively expensive. Trying to reach someone in India from places such as Hong Kong and Singapore—or worse, the United States—took exceptional effort. We were fortunate enough to have a phone in our home, a party line that we shared with at least four other families, so my father was able to get in touch by phone occasionally. Of course, in those days it was necessary to book overseas calls in advance. An operator would call one day and inform us that we would receive a call the next day at a certain time. We would all gather around the phone and wait for my father's call, and we were overjoyed to hear his voice coming from faraway places, telling us about his adventures and checking on our well being.

My father wrote regularly, even though the mails took a long time to reach us. In those days there was no airmail service throughout India, so most of the mail had to come by rail or overland in trucks on roads that made travel slow. International airmail service between London and Bombay began in 1948 but was not available to other countries where my father traveled until the 1950s or later. Additionally, international airmail was expensive, especially for my frugal mother. Nevertheless, my father wrote regularly to assure my mother of his continual concern for all of us, to send money, and to let us know what he was doing. His letters opened my eyes to the wider world and spurred my enthusiasm for the entrepreneur's life.

Once my father was overseas and our uncle's family had settled with us in the house in New Delhi, we established a routine that persisted for nearly a decade. I went to school, studied with a tutor, and played with cousins and friends in the neighborhood. In our large, extended family there were always playmates, and we enjoyed visiting relatives, both my mother's and father's families, who were scattered around the city. Perhaps unconsciously, I was learning how to get along in the adult world by observing my mother and my uncle. I recall an incident that gave me some insight into my mother's character. In those days milk was sold unpasteurized. A milkman would bring the cow to the house and milk it in front of the customer, to prove that he was giving full value for the money. Typically, the milkman would wash the cow's udder before milking, toss out the dirty water from the bucket, and then show the customer that the bucket was empty before beginning to milk. On one occasion my mother caught one of the milkmen adding water to the bucket so the milk would be diluted, and he would make more money. My mother expressed her displeasure vocally! We never saw this milkman in the neighborhood again.

As the oldest male child in our family, it was my job to walk twelve kilometers every other week to get food supplies for the household. On the return trip I would walk with at least fifty pounds of my purchases in my arms and on my back. The Kanard Street Market, a high-end market, was much closer to us, but my mother thought the goods at this market were too expensive. She always sent me to the Bahar Ganj market to get our foodstuffs, except produce, which was sold door-to-door. This open-air bazaar had approximately 1,600 stalls. About half way between home and the bazaar was a candy merchant. In India, candy was sold open and loose, by weight. I would buy candies while I was on this trip and bring them home. My favorite was sugar rock candy. Usually I would hide the candy when I got home to keep it from others and to save it to savor later; unfortunately, I would often forget where I hid it! Days or weeks later my mother would follow a trail of ants to the hidden candy, and I would be punished.

For some reason, from the time I was nine years old until I was eleven I began to fall sick regularly. I thought I had a disease or virus. I was weak all the time, and I would throw up frequently. These ailments put me in a bad position with the neighborhood boys. I was clearly the weakest link in the gang and often was beat up by these so-called friends who would steal whatever I had with me. Although they beat me up, I was taught not to fight back but instead to run away. As a consequence, I had few close friends.

Across the street from our home was a YMCA with open-air basketball courts. We were encouraged to use the facilities whenever we chose. One afternoon I went over to the YMCA to shoot hoops alone. A group of six or seven guys approached. I picked up my ball to go home, but they caught up with me and started a fight, and they were getting the best of me. I do not know what got into me, but I got hold of the leader of this

Jack, age 8, and Davinder, age 5 in front of the YMCA property in New Delhi.

Jack *(standing on top of a two-wheeler)* with *(left to right)* brother Davinder, cousin Kanta Sethi, and sister Purnima.

group and beat him unmercifully. Immediately afterwards I had to throw up badly and then headed home. When I entered our home, my mother asked what had happened. I explained that I had been in a fight. I had always been instructed to walk away from a scuffle, so she punished me. Later, my father, who was in the country at the time, came home from work and my mother told him what had happened. So he punished me. I went to the loft where I slept and went to bed.

Yet, despite all the punishments I felt better physically and mentally. A short while later I went out again. The same guys came around and now accepted me as one of them, and they never picked on me again. But I did not escape scot-free. I was still red from my fighting so the gang nicknamed me "Tomato." I hated that nickname, and to this day I do not eat raw tomatoes!

Curiously, after this fight I was never sick again. I cannot explain why—whether I had overcome some mental block or simply improved—but since then I have never been seriously sick. Call it Providence or Divine Intervention, if you will; all I know is that the incident seemed to cure me of my chronic illnesses.

As I grew older, I gained a great deal of self-confidence and

A family outing in New Delhi showing *(left to right)* **Jack, Purnima, Kanta Sethi, Leela, an aunt with child in arms, and Davinder.**

developed a circle of friends. Many were my own age, but many others were older or younger than I. My sister told me years later that she was envious at times of my popularity, but I simply recall enjoying the opportunity to engage in activities such as cycling, exploring, and playing sports with friends. I especially enjoyed athletics and played soccer and cricket for local teams. Growing up in New Delhi, I was one of thousands of young Indians who aspired to something more than life as a small-time merchant. When I was not yet eleven, I followed with great interest the story of Sir Edmund Hillary's ascent of Mount Everest in 1953. I remember being intrigued by the space race, too, and as a fifteen-year-old celebrating with my fellow students when, in 1957, the Soviet Union became the first nation to put a man in orbit. These events inspired me with a spirit of adventure.

My being a champion of the USSR may need some explanation, but it seems perfectly understandable. At that time India was officially a member of the Nonaligned Nations, a confederation of countries that refused to become too close to either the United States or the Soviet Union during the years of the Cold War. However, from the early days of the new republic, Indian politicians had worked hard to develop a strong relationship with the USSR, and Indian school children were taught that the Soviets were friendly people with whom we should have strong ties. India was not a Communist country, but, like the USSR, had a planned economy and virtual one-party rule, as Congress Party members held a firm majority in the Parliament for decades.

Additionally, because our home was in an upscale neighborhood, we had friends who were influential in the government. Our next-door neighbor was a high-ranking official in the Health Ministry, and we played with his children regularly. Through him, our family received invitations to the Presidential Palace where I remember exchanging greetings with visiting dignitaries, including Soviet leader Nikita Khrushchev and Zhou Enlai, Premier of the People's Republic of China. I attended private schools until I was fifteen, completing my education at Sarswati Maha Vidyalaya, a high school in New Delhi. School was very competitive in those days, and all students scheduled to graduate were required to take a National Board Examination known as the Matriculation Examination. In order to qualify for acceptance into university, one had to pass this exam. This national test was given to all students on a specific day; the results were published in the newspapers. A certain tension hung over students and their families between the day of the examination and the day that results were published; it was common for families to pray frequently and to visit the temple to make offerings to the gods. In the spring of 1958 I took and passed the Matriculation Examination that qualified me for entry into Punjab University. This institution had been founded in 1882 in Lahore, India (now Pakistan), but had relocated to India after the partition of the country. By 1956 it had been re-established in Chandigarh, approximately 150 miles north of our home. I was all set to enroll when we got word that my father had successfully obtained our travel visas to join him in America.

My father had been traveling regularly to the United States where he had begun to set up business contacts. The news that he wanted us to relocate there created a flurry of activity in our household. Obviously, if were to move to America, we would have to learn English. My father, of course, had learned English so he could operate in the business world. But no one else in the family knew English. Our native language was Hindi. That may seem curious, since English was the official language of the country while the British ruled. After India gained independence, however, Hindi became the official language, being designated as such by the Constitution of India adopted in 1950. This fact is not surprising since Gandhi urged Indians to become self-reliant, and maintaining English as the country's language would run counter to that principle. After India gained its independence, schools were no longer required to teach English. As a consequence, I did not receive any instruction in the language while growing up. Therefore, while we waited for my mother and father, with the help of my uncle, to make travel arrangements, we were tutored daily in the English language. I did not find it easy, but I knew I would have to master English in order to adapt to the surroundings in my new homeland.

As things turned out, my father had to go through the visa application process twice. He had arranged for us to join him in America some time before we actually set out for the United States, and we were to make arrangements to set sail from Bombay or Calcutta to New York via Hamburg, Germany. Unfortunately, my mother could not get cheap tickets, and she was unwilling to pay the high prices being demanded for the trip. So we did not leave India, and our visas expired. To his credit, my father went through the application process again. When I was fifteen years old, we were once again ready to depart, visas in hand. A large crowd of family and friends, perhaps as many as a hundred, came to see us off at the train station in New Delhi. This time we were booked on a cargo ship sailing from Bombay, in an underwater cabin. Our initial destination was Southampton, England. From there we sailed on the S.S. Funder to New York, arriving on June 30, 1958.

Those days at sea were some of the worst of my life. The rough motion of the ship caused me to be constantly seasick. I lay on the deck, throwing up what little food I tried to get down. I often wished I would just die. But I knew I would not, so I had to keep suffering. These were not quick trips; each leg took approximately two weeks or more to complete. It seemed an eternity before the ship pulled into port.

Lesson Learned: *When I look back on my youth in India, I realize that, as tumultuous as life there was, my experiences were no different from those of a youngster growing up in New York City or any other large, American city during this same period, who faced poverty, gang violence, and other traumas every day. One can see parallels, too, with African American youngsters growing up in the South, where racial violence shaped their lives in ways similar to what went on in India and Pakistan in 1947. Children are uprooted all the time. What matters is the family structure. If one is lucky, as I was, one can overcome difficult circumstances. In our case, we were fortunate to have strong family bonds. Even though my mother raised us in what was essentially a single-parent household, she had the support of her family, particularly her brother, which proved important for us to maintain family stability in these trying times. My father, too, was there in spirit if not always present physically. He cared deeply for us and supported us financially, and when he was home, he demonstrated his love and concern in a way that made me want to emulate him when I grew up.*

Adjusting to Life in New York City

As the ship's crew began setting the gangway in place for us to disembark in New York, I could see my father on the shore among the large crowd that had gathered for the ship's arrival. Even though we had not seen each other for some time, I recognized him immediately. Perhaps it was "family chemistry," some bond that allows us to identify those whom we love among a crowd of strangers. Each family member had only one suitcase, so I picked up mine and headed down the ramp. We had a family reunion right at the foot of the gangway. My mother allowed each of the children to embrace our father first, while she waited patiently.

Why did my father choose to bring us to this new country? He never told me directly, but I came to understand his decision over time. Naturally, we could have stayed in New Delhi, but that would have meant remaining with my mother's family. We could have emigrated from India to Britain, since the British government had granted all Indians easy immigration to British soil. Many Indians accepted this offer even though they were not immediately granted British citizenship. Of course, the British assumed that only the more well-to-do would move to England because there was no financial support afforded anyone wishing to relocate there. My father decided against this option. In the course of his business, he had traveled all over the world. At one point he had secured a position importing silk from Burma, Thailand, and Singapore into the United States. Apparently he liked what he saw in America and decided to make his home there. After so much travel and separation from the family he felt he could settle down and reestablish a full family life. He believed America offered more opportunities for his family than the divided India in which we were living, or any other place in the world. As best as I can determine, he originally settled in New York City as a permanent resident sometime during 1956, perhaps earlier, and established himself as a successful businessman with the goal of bringing his family to America. Therefore, our arrival in June 1958 must have been a particularly joyous day for him.

When we had finished passing through the immigration center, we headed for our new home in the city. My father had a car, probably one he borrowed from a friend or from his landlord, and we drove to a place he was renting in a residential hotel. The apartment was not large, but it seemed sufficient for our needs. One of our first adjustments was to become accustomed to western methods of hygiene. For example, in India we brushed our teeth with a stick, usually cut from a neem or banyan tree, which we chewed until the end was frayed. Now my father had to teach my siblings and me how to use a toothbrush and toothpaste!

Although the hotel provided maid service once a week, we were probably not good tenants. In India our servants cleaned up for us; in America we had to do everything ourselves, and we were not accustomed to such work. After several months we moved to a permanent apartment on 135th Street. Over time we became more responsible tenants as we learned to adapt to the customs of our new homeland.

Imagine my circumstances as a teenager coming to New York City. I was not familiar with western customs or culture. I had only rudimentary knowledge of English. It was not that I was unaccustomed to living in a big city; New Delhi at the time I left had a population approaching two million. But living there hardly prepared me for what I saw in New York. In 1958 nearly eight million people lived in the city. Tall skyscrapers, many of them built in the post-war boom during the 1950s, blocked the sunlight. Cars and buses crowded the streets. Subways sped along beneath one's feet taking people to and from work or play. The people seemed so free, and relationships between the sexes so much more open and uninhibited than what I had witnessed in India. To my eyes, the women were "exposed," especially compared to Indian women who dressed in saris that went from head to toe. My siblings and I often roamed the streets in awe of what we saw. We were truly overwhelmed and found it difficult to comprehend this new environment that was imposed on us without proper preparation.

While my mother was happy to have reunited with her husband, her adjustment to American life was much more difficult because her roots in India were more established. However, she never complained or openly second-guessed her husband's decision to move to America. She could see that it was best for her children to be with their father and to have the many opportunities available to them in the United States. She took classes and learned to read and write English and eventually went

Jack's parents, Leela and Jagjit Gulati.

to work in my father's store when he needed help. Still, it took my mother a long time to adjust to life in her new homeland. Both my parents were vegetarians; she found it difficult to cook American food. In fact, she continued to cook Indian foods for the rest of her life. Where my father had many friends, my mother had none. The family support system on which she had relied in

India was not available either. Communicating with relatives, especially her brother, on whom she had become dependent during my father's extensive overseas travels, was difficult. Telephone service between the countries was cumbersome to arrange and expensive. Some older ladies in our apartment building befriended her, but there were almost no Indian families in our neighborhood, and few people seemed interested in hearing about India. Eventually, she found some friends from the Hindu temple in Brooklyn where she and my father attended services periodically. It was hard to get to the temple using public transportation, so they did not go every week. One measure of her tenacity to hold onto her Indian identity was that she did not become a naturalized American citizen until 1973.

By contrast, my father received his citizenship in 1961, approximately five years after he established permanent residency. He may have had an easier time adjusting to his adopted country, but he did not abandon the customs he had learned in India. Despite all his world travels, he stayed faithful to his Hindu faith. He prayed every morning and evening. I often saw him praying in Indian fashion, standing erect before a replica of an Indian god with hands pressed together. In

Jack's father, Jagjit Lal Gulati, as a young man in Hindu prayer.

his travels my father had seen widely divergent cultures, and it would have been easy to abandon his past—and his family—and take up with someone else. He had a good job and the resources to set up a new life. But his ethic told him he had an obligation to his wife and children back in India. So instead of falling prey to the temptations of a laissez-faire western culture, he remained faithful to his roots and upheld his responsibilities to us. At this age I was not a very devout person. But I saw that he thought it important to remain true to his traditions. Clearly my father's behavior had an impact on me. I realized that no matter where we end up living, there is a basic DNA inside each of us that keeps us connected to our ancestry.

For my siblings and me, however, life was to be different. My father encouraged us to become westernized. While he and my mother continued to speak Hindi to each other, he demanded that we speak English because it would be our ticket to success in this new environment. It was as if he were telling us, "You are in a new land, and you'll have to make your way here. You must learn the customs and procedures of your new homeland." While it is true that some people who immigrated to America—Indians included—managed to stay within their own ethnic enclaves and be successful, only those who mastered "the American way" of doing things became real successes. I am convinced that my father's encouragement made a real difference in the way I viewed my future in America, even if I did not always acknowledge it at the time.

My father also encouraged us to become familiar with American politics. Sunday afternoons were often spent around the dinner table after an Indian meal discussing the upcoming election. The 1960 contest pitted Democrat John F. Kennedy against Richard M. Nixon, the Republican nominee and current vice president. I remember I was staunchly in favor of Nixon, but not everyone in my family shared my views. My sister and I would sometimes argue over the merits of the candidates or about other political issues. Of course, we were not eligible to vote, but the exercise was an important one for all of us: We were learning about the American way of governing.

During the Nixon Campaign for President, when I was eighteen years old, I got involved in Republican politics in New York City. A local leader took me under his wing and arranged for me to attend the 1960 New York State Republican Convention in Albany. Upon arrival I checked into my hotel room and went to one or two sessions. Somehow I got hold of a bottle of Four Roses whiskey and took it to my room. I had no prior knowledge or experience—no liquor had ever been served in our home— nor had I ever seen adults drinking alcohol. I didn't know that alcohol should be sipped, and I drank the whole fifth of whiskey straight at one sitting. I first passed out and then threw up all over the bed. I don't remember anything from the rest of the day or night. The next afternoon the maid entered the room, saw my drunken, filthy condition in the bed, and put me in a bathtub of water fully clothed. I finally sobered up and somehow found my way home. I never told my parents, but seeing my condition, my father knew that I had been drinking. He talked with me about the incident but never lectured me. It is ironic to me now that my father had once owned liquor stores and yet I was so ignorant of the effects of alcohol.

Eventually we moved to an apartment on Claremont Avenue near 128th Street, close to my father's newly opened hardware store in Harlem. Originally the store had been a gift shop carrying Indian goods, principally religious icons, owned by an Indian immigrant who had decided to return home. He agreed to sell the business to my father who then expanded the business to include hardware. Since it was the only store of its kind in the neighborhood, it provided a decent living for my family. Unlike the import/export business, this line of work allowed my father to stay with his family—something crucial now that we were all in a strange country. In many ways the store was typical of hardware stores located in urban areas, but my father also had a section in which he sold Indian goods—perfumes, candles, ivory figurines, and the like. The neighborhood had long been a population center for the African American community, but by the 1950s the ethnic mix of the neighborhoods once again changed, as more Hispanics moved in. Unfortunately, the mixture of cultures did not always produce harmonious living and working conditions. In 1964 the neighborhood was the site of some of the worst race riots America has ever witnessed. Harlem was always known as a high-crime area; among young people in the area the crime rate approached 50 percent. This sad fact would have great impact on me and my family in the coming years.

Not long after we arrived in New York City, I enrolled in Public School 137 on 137th Street. Even though I had passed the matriculation exam in India, comparable to earning a high-school diploma in America, I was required to enroll in high school because I was only fifteen years old. American education was a great culture shock. The school's population was mostly lower middle class, and my classmates seemed more coarse and worldly-wise than I. Having arrived in the United States only months earlier, I had no idea about American customs. I certainly did not know how to deal with girls or women. That proved a handicap, since I was in class with many girls and had mostly female teachers. I wanted to impress all of them, but they acted as if they could care less about me. Only one, my home room teacher, took an interest in me. I thought I should acknowledge her kindness in some way. In the Indian culture it was customary to bring small presents to teachers. At the time my father was importing ivory goods from India when importation of ivory was legal. My mother gave me a lovely brooch to give to my homeroom teacher, who seemed appreciative.

When not in class I worked at several jobs to earn some spending money. I helped my father in his store when he needed me. For a time I was a runner for a literary agent. My job was to take manuscripts from the agent's office to publishers around town. In those days there was no way to send these documents electronically, and firms did not trust the U.S. mails to deliver time-sensitive materials. Perhaps the most intriguing job I had was as an elevator operator at a high-rise apartment building located at 59th Street and Madison Avenue, a ritzy complex that had its own doorman. I worked the graveyard shift and did not have many calls for service, which was fortunate since I sometimes fell asleep and did not hear the bell that was supposed to alert me to pick up a passenger.

Occasionally I would pretend the elevator had broken down, and that was the reason I did not respond. Fortunately, the residents were polite and understanding and I did not get into trouble. One building tenant, a professional harmonica player who lived on the sixth floor, was accustomed to going out late and coming in during the wee hours of the morning. Sometimes he called for the elevator when I had fallen asleep, and I suspect he knew it, but he never made it an issue. He simply accepted at face value my explanation that the elevator was not working. I remember, too, that a wealthy socialite occupied an apartment on the top floor. She was a divorcee who was having an affair with a married Wall Street banker. He visited frequently, and I received strict instructions on how to treat him and when he would be coming and leaving, so during those times I would make sure I did not fall asleep. The woman was hoping that the man would divorce his wife and marry her. Alas, her hopes were in vain.

My work as an elevator operator gave me my first exposure to unions. As a condition for taking this job I was required to become a member of the Elevator Operators of New York City. Joining this union worked to my advantage. When I began working, I was paid 99 cents an hour; when I joined the union, my wages went up to $1.38 per hour. However, I have never been a great believer in unionization, and even today remain somewhat skeptical about the merits of organized labor. The original purpose of unions—to engage in collective bargaining to negotiate fair wages and working conditions—remains valid. My concern is with the excessive system of rules governing what tasks employees can and cannot perform. For instance, in my position as an elevator operator I had plenty of idle time; yet despite my request to use this time in a productive fashion, I was not permitted to perform other tasks, such as cleaning or mopping the lobby. Such narrow vision, in my experience, often stifles productivity and keeps people from learning new skills that might allow them to advance to positions of greater responsibility and higher earnings. So much idle time probably caused me to fall asleep, deteriorated my performance and inhibited my opportunities to advance.

Because my various jobs left me little time for homework, I was not a very good student. Nevertheless, I graduated high school when I was sixteen years old and applied for admission to City College of New York (CCNY), a part of what is now the City University of New York. I suppose I was admitted because any graduate of a New York City high school was granted admission automatically; hence, there was no real sense of accomplishment in being allowed to begin studies at CCNY. Some of my naiveté about the American educational system can be seen in my response to receiving the acceptance letter. I was disappointed because I was being admitted to "undergraduate study." I was just about to complete high school, and I thought, "How can I be made to go back to being an undergraduate? I am a graduate—I should be going to graduate school!"

Instead of attending CCNY, I took a step that later proved to be one of the smartest things I did in my young life; I enrolled at the RCA Institute to study TV and radio electronics. One could enroll to become a repair technician or pursue a higher level curriculum that provided more advanced technical studies. I took the more advanced course, the Television & General Electronics program, a decision that would end up serving me well in a year or so. I completed the eighteen-month course with good grades and graduated on February 23, 1961. I was eighteen years old.

Leaving Home

When I finished my coursework at the RCA Institute, I thought it would be a good time to leave home. Initially, I thought I would leave New York and go to college in Indianapolis. Unfortunately, I did not communicate my desires well to the travel agent, who booked me to Minneapolis! I stayed in Minneapolis for some time and enrolled at the University of Minnesota for the spring quarter and summer sessions. While there I met fellow student David Young, a talented musician about my age, who wanted to get away from the city. After some late-night discussions we decided to travel back to New York where we might make our fortunes. Therefore, at the end of the summer we headed back East, choosing a highly circuitous itinerary down to Route 66 through the Southwest and back through the Mid-Atlantic States to New York. During this trip I witnessed for the first time outright discrimination against blacks. Seeing separate entrances to restaurants, separate bathrooms and drinking fountains was truly disheartening to Dave and me.

My parents were most happy to see me, and I decided I would now enroll at CCNY. Unfortunately, the experience was not a happy one. CCNY was a big school, and I was decidedly a little fish. While I may have been prepared academically, I was relatively immature and not ready for the environment in which I found myself. No one seemed to care about me. I went for awhile but did not do well and dropped out. I did manage to get a job as an assistant to a buyer of ladies coats and suits with the Independent Retailers Syndicate, an association that represented smaller store chains nationally. I was responsible for distributing flyers to stores to let them know the upcoming line of fashion coats and to take orders.

By the end of spring I had enough of school and was ready to start a career. David Young, who had stayed in New York, was ready for a change as well. We decided we would go to California and pursue acting careers in Hollywood. I told my parents that I was going to leave home for California. In the Indian culture, the notion that a son, especially the eldest son, would leave home was anathema. I was expected to find a young Indian girl, or let my parents find one for me, marry her, and bring her home to live with my family. Unfortunately, at that time I had no interest in marriage, although I did appreciate girls. My mother was totally devastated. How could the eldest son leave home to go so far away? In her mind, California was on the other side of the world.

I was resolute in my decision, however, so David and I set off on our cross-country trek in David's 1957 Ford. This time we headed west on the northern route, toward Minnesota, probably so David could visit his family along the way. We left with minimal money in our pockets. All along the road we pinched pennies, sleeping in the car whenever possible to save cash.

Leela and Jack in front of New York City apartment as Jack sets off for college.

We were leaving Oshkosh, Wisconsin, after a brief stop, and were heading up a hill out of town when the car suddenly began making a clicking noise and stopped running. I knew nothing about cars, and David knew only slightly more. We turned the car around and coasted back into town to a garage we had seen earlier. The mechanic took a look and gave us the bad news: we had a blown engine. In all likelihood, he said, we had run out of oil. "What will repairs cost?" we asked naively. "$647.60," was the answer. I was astounded. "Come on," I said. "We do not have that kind of money." I remembered that I had recently left my family crying; there was little likelihood that they would send funds to bail us out. We asked if we could leave the car and come back when we had the money. The mechanic agreed.

In those days it was still possible to hitchhike. David and I headed back out to the highway and stuck out our thumbs. We were picked up by an older gentleman who asked where we were heading. We told him we were on our way to California. He said he was heading for Minneapolis and would be happy to drive us that far. We decided to take him up on his offer. The trip went uneventfully, and our driver dropped us off on University Avenue, right in the heart of the University of Minnesota's fraternity row. It was summer, and students were away. A sign in the window of the Delta Chi fraternity house read: ROOM AND BOARD, $10.00 A WEEK, INCLUDING THREE MEALS DAILY. The deal was too good to pass up, so David and I took rooms there.

Being back on campus got me thinking about college again. Soon, I found I had an important decision to make. David managed to get his hands on enough money to ransom his car. I made up my mind to stay in Minneapolis and re-enroll at the University. Fortunately for me, the University had two summer sessions that offered open enrollment at the in-state tuition rate. My parents were willing to help out financially with tuition and board. I decided to enroll immediately. I took a couple of classes and, on the strength of my performance at the RCA Institute, got a job in the Electrical Engineering Department as a technician.

I already knew I wanted to be an engineer, so I went to the Dean and asked if I could enroll in the Electrical Engineering program in the University's Institute of Technology. When school officials looked at my transcripts from high school and CCNY, they said, "No way." However, I was permitted to enroll in the two-year General College—no great shakes, as every Minnesota high-school graduate had a right to enroll in that college. Because I had the good fortune to have a job at the University and a Minneapolis address, I was allowed to enroll at the in-state tuition rate for the regular quarter at a cost of $240.00 compared to nearly $660.00 per quarter for out-of-state students. I was happy with the situation, but I really did not do justice to my schoolwork. I enjoyed partying and fraternity life, even though I never pledged. To make matters worse, most campus activities, including football games and homecoming, took place around mid-quarter, and I was not going to let academics get in the way of a good time. Typically I would find myself with D or F grades at midterm; then I would buckle down and study hard for the remainder of the quarter and bring my grades up to C.

After a couple of years I matured and decided to get serious about my studies. I went to my advisor to see how I might pursue an engineering degree. I began doing better in my classes and managed to get out of General College with grades sufficiently high to allow me to enroll in the Electrical Engineering Program at the Institute of Technology, a five-year program.

I was a reasonably frugal person at this point. From every paycheck I would take money and purchase five silver dollars and save this money to buy a plane ticket home. My parents seemed to like this plan, and I returned to their good graces. I also continued working summers in Minneapolis. One summer I got a job with a traveling circus that was setting up in town. I enjoyed the physical labor, although it was hard. Apparently I did a good job because I was asked if I wanted to accompany the troop when they left town. "It'll be great for a young guy like you," one of the circus hands told me. "Look at me. I've got a girl in every town!" Fortunately, I did not fall for this enticement and instead stayed in college.

The people for whom I was working in the Electrical Engineering department liked me, even though I was not always adept at setting up experiments for the professors and graduate students. Despite my determination, however, I did not do particularly well in the electrical engineering curriculum. I decided I was not going to make it as an engineer. At this time computers were becoming an exciting and popular new field of study, and I discovered that I liked working with them. I learned that one did not need an Electrical Engineering degree to work on computers, so I switched my major to Mathematics, largely because I was getting good grades in math.

But that was not the end of my academic maneuvering. I discovered that if I stayed in the Institute of Technology to pursue a Mathematics degree, I would commit to a five-year program; by contrast, a Mathematics degree from the College of Liberal Arts could be completed in four years. I changed colleges and was able to finish my required coursework more quickly. I should point out, however, that although I had substantially completed the requirements for an undergraduate degree, and walked across the stage in my cap and gown in 1964, I did not get my official degree at that time. I continued my studies for awhile, hoping I would eventually pursue a Master's Degree, but soon found it impossible to continue in school and work full-time. So I paid my fees and fines and received my degree in 1966.

Jack's graduation photo from the University of Minnesota, 1964.

A final note about my college years: almost as soon as I had arrived in America, I had completed a "Declaration of Intent" indicating my desire to become an American citizen. The waiting period to become a naturalized citizen was five years. So while I was in Minnesota in 1963, I applied for my American citizenship. On February 13, 1964 I became a naturalized American citizen. At that time I officially changed my name from Ashok Kumar Gulati to Jack David Gulati. I was ready to set out on my journey to realize the American Dream.

PART II

Building a Successful Career

Although I was not yet officially a college graduate, in 1964, having completed my course work, I went to work in the research lab for The Minnesota Mining & Manufacturing Company (later 3M), in Hastings, Minnesota. My job was to conduct research on various resins used in the manufacture of plastic. It was a good job, but I did not stay long. I thought my new "Uncle"— Uncle Sam—might be asking me to go to work for him, and I was not thrilled about the kinds of jobs he was offering.

Jack in Air Force ROTC uniform at the University of Minnesota, circa 1961.

Let me explain. In 1964, the war in Vietnam was going strong. I had joined the Air Force Reserve Officer Training Corps (ROTC) at the university with the goal of becoming a pilot and pursuing a career in the military. Unfortunately, sometime after I enrolled, I learned that I was color blind, and therefore could not qualify to be a pilot. I was told I might qualify as a navigator, but I was hardheaded and decided not to continue the program. It was "pilot or nothing" for me. That may have been an unwise decision. During the time I was in college I had received a student deferment. Now that I was no longer in school, I was eligible to be drafted into the U.S. Army. In a few months my draft board in New York would enter my name in the draft lottery. I knew I had to do something if I wanted to avoid being drafted.

Employment at Univac Defense Systems

I landed a new job with Univac Defense Systems, a division of Sperry Rand, in St. Paul, Minnesota in the field services division. At the time Sperry Rand's Univac Defense Systems Division was a major supplier of computer systems to the Department of Defense. Univac sent me through nine months of training classes. I learned programming, design, repair and maintenance—all the skills I needed to be a competent technician. I was then assigned to upgrade computers for the Gemini and Apollo space programs. The job took me to Hawaii, North Carolina, Florida, Alaska, and North Dakota. Not only did I enjoy the travel and the work, but Univac also helped me get a new deferment from the draft; my present position classified my work as critical to the defense effort.

After working on the space programs for approximately a year, I was assigned to Univac's Design & Product Improvement Field Service Team for the Stealth Bomber radar. It was the Air Force's most innovative program at the time. Hughes Aircraft and Univac had the contract to design the computer system for the

Jack working on the Army computer at Univac, his first job.

program. In 1966 the company sent me to California, the place I had set out for several years earlier.

California was experiencing wild times. It was the era of "topless" everything. I lived in Inglewood, near Los Angeles International Airport. My apartment complex was a cinderblock structure that circumscribed a swimming pool. I rented an apartment with another fellow but soon became disenchanted with the pretentiousness I saw all around me. People seemed willing to go to extremes to try to impress each other. For example, at this time cars with air conditioning were becoming more available, but many people could not afford this luxury. However, some drivers drove in the California hot sun with their windows rolled up, pretending that they had air conditioning. I quickly realized that this kind of pretentiousness was foolish. And the ploy did not work well anyway. If you looked closely at these drivers, you could penetrate the façade; they were simply pretending to have more than they really did.

That is not to say I was immune from status-seeking. In 1965 I bought a jet black Mustang convertible—actually a 1964½, as the company introduced its new model in mid-year. The price was slightly below $2,400.00. As an aside, I might mention it was the only car I ever bought on credit; my monthly payments were approximately $73.00. It was a car that made people's heads turn. One day while the car was parked outdoors, the area experienced a horrific hail storm. When I came outside, I noticed that my car had suffered numerous dents all over. I checked with my insurance company and learned that I could have the dents repaired and the car repainted at no cost to me. When I took it to the body shop, I asked that the new paint job be white rather than black. That way it would appear that I had a new car.

Lesson Learned: *Paying interest on car payments taught me a lifelong lesson. I was putting money in someone else's pocket and getting nothing in return. So when the note was paid off in three years, I kept "paying myself," putting into savings the amount I had been paying on the car. Three years later I was able to buy my next car with cash. It is not wise to buy a depreciating asset on credit. Of course, one needs certain items to make life easy: automobiles, washers and dryers, and the like. Buying these big-ticket items on credit is normal. Still, it is best to save for these and avoid purchasing on credit. When I have needed a major item, I have paid cash. If that meant I had to buy a used one rather than a new one, so be it. I also determined that I would not use credit to purchase items that have no lasting value—meals, for example. That does not mean I do not use credit cards; but if I do, I pay off the bill when it comes due rather than let interest pile up.*

I had another experience while I was in California that also taught me a valuable lesson. Shortly after settling down in my new surroundings, I got interested in the stock market. At that time I did not realize that investors made money over time and that speculators almost always lost money. However, brokers always made money on the transaction fees. The New York Stock Exchange opened at 9:30 a.m. Eastern Standard Time—6:30 a.m. in California. Early each morning I went to the offices of Kidder Peabody where a ticker tape board showed real-time trading activities. At any time of the day there were a dozen or more other individuals also watching the tape. I would hang out at Kidder Peabody until it was time to go to work, spend the morning at the office, then go back at lunch hour to see the closing hour of the market (from 3:00 – 4:00 p.m. EST). I was fascinated and began playing the market. I lost some money and then made some. Of course, my broker was happy because I was buying and selling regularly, trying to outsmart the market—and he was getting his commissions whether I was winning or losing. I was not an investor; I was a speculator, a day trader before day-trading became popular with the advent of computer trading.

At the time, stocks could be purchased on a 65 percent margin—sometimes 75 percent—meaning I had to put up only 35 percent (or in some cases only 25 percent) of the value of the stock. Convertible bonds were the "hot" new financial instruments. They acted like bonds but traded as stocks; so one was able to take the bond and convert it to the company's stock at a predetermined price. As stocks rose, the bond's value rose with it. When stock went down, the convertible bond acted as a bond and paid interest. Eventually, my broker introduced me to convertible bonds. What made these financial instruments even more attractive was that some could be purchased on a 95 percent margin, meaning one had to put up only 5 percent of the purchase price. This all sounded good to me, so I decided to invest in convertible bonds.

The financial markets were undergoing notable changes. Some entrepreneurs began to form conglomerates, buying up individual companies and selling shares in the parent company. Others realized that individual components of these conglomerates were worth more individually than the entire conglomerate. One of the pioneers in this type of trading was Jim Ling, who eventually founded Ling-Temco-Vought. Ling would buy conglomerates, split them into components, and sell the individual business unit to the public, in an Initial Public Offering (IPO). Every time there was an IPO for one of these companies, I would make a purchase. This kind of investment made sense to me. However, I was unaware of a crucial maneuver being practiced by the firms who were responsible for creating a market for these kinds of shares. For a short period of time after the IPO, the underwriting firms were responsible for providing a stabilized market for the just-released shares by keeping supply and demand of these shares in balance. If there were excessive sellers of the stock, the underwriters would buy the shares for their own inventory, and the reverse would be true if there were excessive buyers. Hence, the value of the stock almost always rose after the initial IPO. When the underwriting firms were no longer responsible for providing this stabilization and released their shares, the stock would often go down. The pros knew this, but I did not. My broker was happy to see me buy IPOs because he was making a fixed commission on all my trades. I would typically buy an IPO and then sell as soon as it went up a few points. By sheer luck I was following a speculation strategy that made a little profit. Of course, the broker made a steady income from my activity but had little interest in my well-being. Still, in my initial trading in these kinds of offerings, I made money and saw no reason to back away from what seemed like a sure thing.

I learned the downside of this form of trading when I became an investor in Control Data Corporation (CDC). The convertible bonds on the initial offering for CDC had a margin of 95 percent, meaning I had to put down only 5 percent of the bond's value. I had accumulated some money, so I put up $50,000 to purchase $1,000,000 CDC convertible bonds. I was proud to have saved this much money, and thought I was on my way to financial success. My experience had led me to believe that, in almost all cases, IPOs went up. But that did not happen in this case. Much to my chagrin, the stock went down, so the bond also went down in value. In three days my entire equity of $50,000 was wiped out. Typically, one has three days to deliver the money for the stocks one has purchased. My broker called to tell me I had to come up with significantly more money to cover the margin call. I did not have any money left to cover this margin call, so my CDC bonds were automatically sold at a significant loss.

My salvation came through a combination of luck and careful maneuvering. The day after I learned how much I would have to pay on my CDC margin call, I saw that a new IPO, Maryland Cup Corporation convertible bonds, was being issued. Although I had no money to pay for this new purchase, I figured I had three days to figure out how to get the money if I were to put in an order to buy $1,000,000 in Maryland Cup's newly issued offering. Again I was lucky; my purchase order was executed. By a further stroke of luck, Maryland Cup went up in value—up high enough to cover all my losses on CDC and allow me to make a decent profit, so I sold my Maryland Cup convertible bonds. Of course, I could not get the proceeds from the sale of the Maryland Cup bonds until I paid for them, and I had no money. Nevertheless, I felt I ought to be able to find a way out of this financial predicament.

My plan was this: I gave Kidder Peabody a check drawn on my account at the University Bank in Minneapolis to cover the CDC losses and to purchase the newly-issued Maryland Cup bonds. Unfortunately, there was no money in the account to cover this check because I had been wiped out. That night I flew back on the red-eye to Minneapolis. The bank manager there knew me fairly well because I had done business with him from my early days as a student at the University of Minnesota, and had maintained my banking relationship with the bank. In those days checks were cleared manually, so it was not uncommon for payees to have to wait a few days before the bank on which a check was drawn would actually release the money. So I asked the bank manager to hold the check for a few extra days, assuring him that my profits from Maryland Cups would cover the check. Fortuitously, he agreed. Since my Maryland Cup bonds had already been sold at a profit, I received a check from Kidder Peabody. In those days there were no "next day" delivery services, so I flew back to Minneapolis to make a deposit to cover my original check to Kidder Peabody. The bank manager told me that he considered holding the check to be a short-term loan, so I had to buy him a dinner. I made a handsome profit on the transaction. In fact, I doubled my net worth. But I had learned my lesson; this was the last market transaction that I ever bought on margin.

Lesson Learned: *Although the Federal Reserve Board's rules for buying on margin have been tightened in recent years, and it is now unlikely that one could buy any stock or bond with only 5 percent down, it is still important to remember* *that buying stocks and bonds on high margin must be done very carefully. It sounds enticing to know that an investment of $50,000 on a 95 percent margin can allow you to control an investment value of $1 million dollars. If the investment instrument (stock or bond) increases by a mere 5 percent, you will have doubled your investment. On the other hand, if the investment instrument drops by 5 percent your entire investment (in my example, $50,000) will be wiped out, as the instrument will be automatically sold by your broker. This scenario applies to any investment on margin; when the value of your investment instrument goes up, you stand to make good money, but if it decreases in value, you can easily lose everything you have invested—and in some cases, even owe your broker additional money. The bottom line is that you need to educate yourself about the market before you invest, and you must keep abreast of changes that affect your investments. Even when you understand the instruments in which you are investing, you must be willing to take some risk, as nothing is guaranteed.*

While learning by hard-won experience the vagaries of the stock market, I continued to work for Univac on the Stealth bomber contract. By this point, however, I had discovered that Southern California was not a family-friendly place, and that it was filled with too many phony people interested only in status. After being in Southern California for about a year, I was certainly not disappointed that Univac called me back to Minneapolis.

When I returned to the Univac offices in Minnesota, I was asked what I wanted to do. I suggested that the company do some additional research in developing a mini-computer that would be both functional and aesthetically pleasing. Company officials were intrigued, and they gave me time to work on the project. I completed the task, but my recommendations were not adopted. To this date, I think Univac missed the boat by not following up on my suggestions since minicomputers proved to be the next generation of computers. I then left Univac and took a job with EMR Computer; a manufacturer in the budding minicomputer industry that I thought had more promise.

Family Matters:
Happiness and Tragedy

Shortly after returning to Minneapolis, I married Nancy Owen, whom I had met at the University of Minnesota before I went to California. She was the daughter of a doctor at the Mayo Clinic in Rochester, Minnesota. We had dated for several years while we were in college. I had brought her to my sister Purnima's wedding to Leon Thomsen in 1965 to meet my family. We were married on June 24, 1967 at a church ceremony attended by both families. Unfortunately, I was probably too immature for married life. I was hesitant to open up to Nancy. This may have sown the seeds for what would happen several years later, when the two of us were under great personal stress and living on the East Coast, far away from her family. However, after we married, Nancy and I set up our home in Minneapolis.

Minnesotans enjoy the outdoors when the weather permits, and I found it easy to adapt to this lifestyle. When we were not working, Nancy and I enjoyed pup-tent camping. In late July 1967 we set off on a week-long trip into the Minnesota

Leon and Purnima's wedding photo, From left: Leon, Purnima, Leela and Jagjit.

wilderness. The trip was enjoyable and uneventful, but as we emerged from the trail, we were met by a Park Ranger who asked my name. He said that people had been looking for me all week. I was to call home immediately.

I reached my mother in New York who told me that my father had been shot and killed in a robbery at his hardware store. On July 29, 1967 the New York Times carried a brief notice of his murder, reporting that two young men entered the store and demanded money. My father did not take them seriously and insisted that they leave. But they did not go quietly, and this miscalculation cost him his life. The Times story reported that my father had chased the robbers as they left the store and was shot by one of them as they fled. They were never captured. To make matters worse, my mother had been at the store at the time and witnessed the entire event.

While my father's murder received little notice in New York, it was front-page news almost immediately in New Delhi. Newsboys hawking papers traveled up and down the streets of our old neighborhood shouting, "Gulati killed in New York City!" My relatives bought copies of the paper and learned the tragic details of my father's death. My mother received phone calls and letters from her family in India and elsewhere. Hence, it was possible to take some comfort in knowing that we had the support of family at this trying time.

Nevertheless, the incident left my mother shaken and frightened. She had seen the robbers, and she knew they had seen her. She refused to remain in her Claremont Avenue apartment for fear that they would come after her. She moved in with my sister and her husband on 113th Street. For several months she and my brother Davinder slept in the living room of the Thomsen's one-bedroom apartment. Any noise at the door horrified my mother. To make matters worse, she had no real support network in New York. She began going to the Presbyterian Church on 110th Street regularly for comfort, even though she remained a Hindu. She was not willing to go back to the store after my father's murder, so the store remained closed. However, my father was well known in that area; many of his customers left flowers and other mementos in front of the store.

Purnima, Davinder, and I had to retrieve all personal items from the establishment and then try to sell the business. We worked with a broker who helped find a buyer. The deal closed in December 1967. Unfortunately, at the time we were not very savvy about property transactions. We agreed to let the buyer pay us over five years. After two small payments, we never saw another dime. I suspect the new owner simply went into the store and took out all the merchandise, leaving the property abandoned.

My mother was left with no significant means of support, and there was only minimal insurance. New York City had a fund available to compensate victims of violent crimes, but my mother was denied compensation, and we decided not to pursue the matter further. The entire affair left my mother broken-hearted, and she never really recovered.

After my mother and Davinder were settled with Purnima and Leon in their apartment, I returned to Minneapolis. Purnima and Leon took mother back to India in 1968 so she could place my father's ashes in the Ganges River, as was the Indian custom. She remained in India with her brother and sisters for three months, but she returned to New York to be closer to her children.

Lesson Learned: *Looking back with the benefit of hindsight, I have come to realize that the loss of my father was a more significant blow to my personal and professional life than I might have realized back then. I was only twenty-three at the time of his murder; I was recently married and just starting my career. In my early years I had relied on him for advice. Clearly, my father, who was an experienced business entrepreneur and devoted family man, could have played an* *important role as a counselor in both areas. He was a man of honor and integrity. He had been popular and well liked in India and New York City, known for his respectful treatment of people rich and poor. He would have been an ideal role model.*

After my father's death I had no one like him to whom I could turn for advice. My mother was a wonderful woman, but her life experience did not equip her to provide guidance regarding my business activities. While it is true that, over the years, I benefited from the sage counsel of various mentors, I am certain that, had my father lived, I would have begun my career as an entrepreneur much earlier than I did, and may well have been more successful in my initial efforts. Simply put, he was irreplaceable.

Moving to Pennsylvania

Back in New York, my mother's life was not easy. Most of my parents' wealth had been tied up in their business. Because my mother was unable to realize anything from that enterprise, she suffered financially. Although she did not ask me directly, it soon became clear that she wanted me to come home. I started to search for employment opportunities in and around New York City. I inquired at my former employer, Univac Defense Systems, to see if I could be transferred to Univac's Commercial Division located in Blue Bell, Pennsylvania, which I thought was sufficiently close to New York to allow me to rejoin the company and be near my mother. Unfortunately, I was turned down. Defense budgets were being reduced as the war in Vietnam was winding down, and the Univac Defense Systems' business was affected by these cuts. Many people within the company were asking for transfers to the Commercial Division. However, I was assured that, if I moved to the area and applied directly for a position with Univac Commercial Division, I would in all probability be hired.

I was in luck, however. EMR, my present employer, had recently been bought out by Varian, a medical instruments company that was just getting into the minicomputer business very similar to the one I had proposed to Univac. The firm agreed to transfer me to the Philadelphia area where I opened an office and became East Coast Regional Sales Manager. Nancy and I moved in the spring of 1968.

We first rented a farmhouse near Lansdale. Pennsylvania. A year later, in August 1969, we bought our first home in King of Prussia. Now that I was living outside Philadelphia, I was close enough to visit New York regularly to check on my mother and my brother, Davinder. I did my best to help out from a distance, but Purnima and Leon provided the lion's share of the care. I went up on weekends to do what I could. My visits were very important to my mother, who always respected the old-country tradition of relying on the eldest son. Nancy never complained about my having to support my mother. In the summer of 1968 we took mother to Europe and toured Greece, Spain and Italy. The trip was fun for us, and it was especially important for me to help my mother overcome her grief.

The sorrow that accompanied my father's death was also eased by events in my own family life. On October 24, 1969 Nancy and I were blessed by the birth of our first child, Jack David Gulati II. The birth of her first grandson lifted my mother's spirits immensely. She immediately visited us and remained for several weeks helping Nancy and me adjust to parenthood.

Despite what help I could provide, the situation was difficult for Purnima because, in addition to having my mother live with her, she also had my brother Davinder, a fine person who was afflicted, tragically, by mental illness. When he was diagnosed, the family was caught completely off-guard. Davinder had been a normal little brother, perhaps the smartest of the three siblings. He certainly got the best grades in elementary and high school. He won his high school's mathematics competition and represented the school in citywide competition. After graduating from high school, he enrolled in the City College of New York. Unfortunately, shortly after he turned eighteen, he was diagnosed with schizophrenia, and much later with bipolar disorder. My father was still alive then, and both he and my mother were crushed by the news. Nevertheless, they did the best they could to take care of him. The doctors recommended that he be placed in Bellevue Hospital, reputed to be a leading center for psychiatric care. Later, on the recommendation of the doctors at Bellevue, he was moved to a facility in upstate New York. My parents were not experts on these matters, so they concurred with the doctors' advice. Sadly, they discovered that my brother was simply being warehoused with other patients and was not receiving the kind of individual attention he needed. I am certain that, had they known better, they would have made any sacrifice necessary to give him better treatment.

Davinder was institutionalized for some time, but his situation was altered dramatically when the national policy on the treatment of the mentally ill changed. In 1963, Congress passed the Community Mental Health Act. The aim of the legislation was to fund the establishment of community-based care for those with mental illnesses and to eliminate the need for large institutions at which care for these individuals had traditionally been provided. As a consequence, many large facilities were shut down, and patients were placed back in the community, predominately in smaller group homes. Sadly, patients who could not get into the few group homes that were available were forced to live with family and receive care on an outpatient basis. My brother was one of those individuals. He returned home and lived with my parents. My father worked six days a week but devoted whatever time he had, particularly on Sundays, to Davinder's care. After my parents returned from the Hindu temple, they would often take him to the zoo, park, or on other outings. Staying home for six days a week did not help my brother combat his illness, but the arrangement was the best my parents could make at the time. Naturally, when my father died, my mother became sole caretaker of Davinder, and he went with her to live with Purnima and Leon.

After sharing space in their tiny apartment with my mother and brother for several months, Purnima and Leon moved to a new place just two blocks away. My mother and Davinder remained in the apartment on 113th Street near Broadway. It was a safe location, so it made sense for them to remain there. Davinder moved in with Purnima and Leon for a time, but moved back with my mother when the Thomsens moved to Paris in 1969 when Leon accepted a teaching assignment abroad.

Divorce and Its Aftermath

Though I had been quite willing to move back East to help my mother, my relocation to Philadelphia did not go well at first. My family circumstances weighed heavily on me, and as a result, I was not a very good sales manager for Varian. A year after I joined the company I received notice that my draft-exempt status had been revoked because I was no longer working in the defense industry. I went to the Draft Board for an interview and then applied for and was granted a "Head of Household" deferment. Shortly thereafter the United States abolished the draft, and I was never called. I often wonder what would have happened if I had been drafted or if I had not dropped out of the Reserve Officer Training Corps. I would not have objected to being in the military, but I would have wanted to be an officer. Had I gone to Vietnam, my life would certainly have been different.

Sometime later I called an associate with whom I had worked at Univac in Minnesota. He was now with Univac Commercial Division in Blue Bell, Pennsylvania, and he put me in touch with the right people at the company and recommended me for a position. In March 1969 I was hired as a salesman. At first I did a good enough job and was promoted to Medical Industry Sales Manager for the Philadelphia area, but my mind was still on my family, and I was never a top performer. In June 1970 I was terminated.

One of the main reasons for my discomfort at this time was my home life. Nancy and I began to have petty squabbles. Curiously, money was not an issue. Even though I was unemployed, I still had enough money to pay our bills, but my being out of work may have put additional strain on our marriage. The birth of our second son, Charles Jagjit Gulati, another joyous event on November 12, 1970, suppressed our differences for a time, but eventually our petty arguments resurfaced. I was always upset with her smoking, and she would sneak around to light up behind my back. Nancy took a job outside the home as a social worker, something that should not have surprised me, as she was very bright and had a degree in psychology. Finally, after yet another argument with Nancy, I left the house and rented a room in Philadelphia. I did not call home for three days. When I did ring, I got no answer then or for the next two days. I finally reached Nancy's parents who assured me that she and the boys were safe. Nancy and a male co-worker, James Wesley (Wes) Fisher, had gone to California with the boys, but then returned to Pennsylvania after a brief stay.

When Nancy came back, I attempted to reconcile, but she was adamant that she wanted a divorce. To her credit, we reached an amicable settlement in a very short time, without significant disagreements. The boys were to live with her, but we had joint custody, which allowed me to have them every other weekend and at other times by mutual consent. Because I was drawing unemployment, my child support payments were set low. Nancy could have sought more when I started working again, but she did not. She got a good job as a statistical analyst for a market research firm. The boys stayed with a sitter each day while Nancy went to work. Eventually, she married Wes, and he became a caring stepfather for my sons.

In many ways, ours was a textbook divorce. We each had lawyers, of course, but we decided we would be in charge of the process and make decisions about both the property and the children. We used the attorneys to implement our wishes. Our divorce was finalized on December 14, 1971.

After a period of unemployment, I secured a good job. Because my child support payments were reasonable, when I went back to work I was able to save quite a bit as I started making good money. I used some of the money to buy the boys whatever they needed. I promised Nancy that I would pay for the boys' healthcare, and their college educations, as well as take care of other major needs. I must give Nancy credit for her part in a very reasonable divorce and for being accommodating, so that we could raise our two sons mutually. On my part, I made certain she received her child support payments on time, and when, from time to time, she needed extra financial assistance, I was always ready to help.

Sadly, sometime in the early 1990s, Nancy discovered she had breast cancer. Her illness caused her to miss work. Eventually she became wheelchair-bound, and then bedridden. When she was on her deathbed, she sent for me. She expressed regret that our marriage did not work out and told me she experienced great joy in seeing all I had done for the boys. I told her I was also sorry that things had turned out as they did, but I said I thought she was the one who should be proud of the boys, since she was the major force behind their upbringing when they were young. She asked me to continue to care for them, and I, of course, agreed. The next day, on April 15, 1998, she died. I think she died in peace. Wes continued to be on good terms with our family, especially with the boys, who accepted him as their stepfather.

My divorce provided me some important lessons about myself and about differences between Indian and American cultures. As a first generation immigrant from India, I was particularly taken aback at the idea of divorce. In New Delhi, where I had lived for more than a decade, there had been only a handful of divorces each year among a population exceeding one million. While that circumstance has changed radically today, in 1971 I still believed that marriage was to last forever. In retrospect, though, my divorce from Nancy, while not inevitable, could have been predicted. During the 1970s the divorce rate in the United States increased by 40 percent. Sociologists have suggested a number of reasons for the spike. Supported by the women's movement, many young women like Nancy decided they did not want to be stay-at-home moms, and they entered the work force. While seeking work outside the home may have been both right and laudatory, many husbands had a difficult time adjusting to the idea that their wives were going to be career women. Interestingly, a second reason why we may have been more likely than other couples to divorce was Nancy's habit of smoking. In the 1970s no one might have thought that smokers were more likely to divorce than non-smokers, but research conducted in the 1990s provides strong evidence that such is the case. Unfortunately, we did not realize these factors were working against us.

I do not want to suggest that Nancy and I overcame our differences quickly. We had our share of arguments, but I do not ever remember them involving the boys. In this I was extremely lucky, but I think the seeds for our conciliatory relationship going forward were sown at the time of our divorce when we did not argue over terms. We certainly did not have much to split up, but as it turned out, I received the house. It was not a home, however, as my boys and the items that might have brought back memories all went with Nancy.

Lesson Learned: *Even an event as traumatic as divorce and its aftermath can provide lessons to those willing to step back and consider what happens when two people decide to part ways. I believe it is possible to identify three stages that occur when one gets divorced. The first is an emotional time: you are angry, mad at the world and especially at the spouse who no longer wants you and whom you may no longer want. However, at the same time, you may believe you can reconcile differences and get your life back to the way it used to be. Second comes a time of acceptance when the fact of divorce sets in. You know that you will have to go on with your life without your partner; you may remarry or not, but in either case you will have to get used to the fact that the old way of life is gone forever. Third comes a time for adjustment—at least it can come if both parties work at it. A successful settlement allows you to come to accept what has happened, make up with the person who caused you so much heartache, and move on— even, perhaps, restore an amicable relationship. One thing you cannot do is wallow in self-pity or let yourself be eaten up by guilt; nor can you spend time and energy blaming your former partner for what went wrong. No matter how painful divorce can be, you must focus on the future and determine how you will live the rest of your life, not how you should have lived in the past.*

Remarriage and New Successes in Business

My employment history after Nancy and I initially separated can best be described as a series of promising starts, most of which ended up leading nowhere. I never let an opportunity pass by to become involved with ventures that I thought had promise. The opportunity now presented itself for me to take risks and set out on my path to become an entrepreneur. In January 1971 I started Medical Computer Services, to provide more rapid and accurate billing services to doctors and clinics. Even though the concept was good and well thought out, the project went nowhere because I had neither the financial resources to pay to develop the software, nor the time to develop it myself. I ended up shutting down the business four months later. Earlier in the year I had taken a job with the Ross Bureau of Investigation as a night watchman to bring in some extra income, and by April 1971 I had landed a position with Ex-Cell-O Computer Products.

I fared much better in my personal life. I visited my mother more frequently, and got back into the social scene. In March

1972, I attended a dance where I met Rosemary Murphy, a schoolteacher in the Cheltenham School District. She impressed me immediately as a very fine and sincere person, and we hit it off immediately. I shared my story with her, including the fact that I had been married and had two sons. Within a few months after we met, I took her to New York to meet my mother, who accepted her immediately.

At Ex-Cell-O I became Regional Sales Manager. My job was to market new computer hardware. The Detroit-based company had established a Computer Products Division at its manufacturing plant in Walled Lake, Michigan, where

Rosemary's graduation photo from Chestnut Hill College, 1961.

highly sophisticated grinding machines created disk drive platters that were magnetized so they could interface with IBM computers to store data. The business concept was to provide IBM-compatible disk drives at a reduced price. Initially, the concept worked well, and several companies like Memorex became competitors. I saw a niche open up for Ex-Cell-O to provide similar devices for RCA computers. At the time RCA was still a major supplier of mainframe computers. Based on my business plan, the company decided to enter this market.

Having a more stable personal life allowed me to concentrate on work. In concert with the staff at Ex-Cell-O's office in

Cherry Hill, New Jersey, I managed to land a large contract with Fidelity Bank of Philadelphia. This multi-million-dollar deal was the largest in the company's history. Our engineers worked diligently on this program for a year, and I provided customer interface. Unfortunately, product delivery lagged six months behind. On the other hand, when we finally delivered the disks and installed them, they passed operational tests. I brought my team back to my home to celebrate, but our jubilation was short-lived. Shortly after we installed the new system at the bank, Ex-Cell-O announced that it was getting out of the disk drive business. The company took a loss because the disks had to be removed and damages paid. I often wonder if company engineers had developed the product six months earlier, and we had installed the product on time, if management would have still chosen to shut down operations. Ex-Cell-O treated me fairly, and I was the last person to turn off the lights at the East Coast office.

Once again I was looking for work, but I was not too worried. I had sideline employment as a representative for two high-tech firms, Computer Solutions and DIVA Inc., helping to market their products. I also was part owner of Entry Equipment Limited and a partner in Market Study Associates. In addition, I became affiliated with Triester International Investments, a money management firm in Philadelphia. While none of these jobs seemed to have a long-term future, they carried me through until I landed a full-time position with Inforex Inc., another computer products manufacturer, in 1973.

By this time my relationship with Rosemary Murphy had become serious, and I finally asked her to marry me. My mother always had concerns about David and Chuck, and after we became engaged, my mother told Rosemary that she had prayed that I would marry a teacher because teachers have to love all children. My second marriage taught me the importance of honoring people's religious traditions. First, we planned to be married in July; however, at my mother's request, we postponed the date to August, as she observed the month of July as a mourning period for my father. Second, before we could be married, I had to obtain an annulment of my first marriage from the Catholic Church. I was happy to go through this process because it was important to Rosemary. We experienced some delays while the appropriate paperwork was assembled and submitted, but the process was not particularly difficult.

Jack and Rosemary's wedding on August 11, 1973. Pictured left to right are Rosemary's parents, Daniel A. and Mary R. Murphy, Rosemary and Jack, Leela Gulati, Leon and Purnima Thomsen. *(Photo by Walter Free Studios)*

Rosemary and I married on August 11, 1973. She immediately accepted my sons as her own, and became their second mother. The boys called her "Mare," an appropriate nickname for "Mary" that sounds like the French word for "Mother." Two years later we experienced another blessed event: Michael Eric Gulati was born on June 26, 1975. We made sure Michael knew he had two brothers, even though they lived at another place most of the time when they were young. The three boys enjoyed activities together, and there was never a feeling among the boys that they belonged to separate families. David and Chuck had a complete wardrobe at our home, so they were not made to feel like "suitcase children" shuffling back and forth between homes. Eventually, any hurt that remained after my divorce from Nancy wore off, and the two families together dealt amicably with issues regarding the boys.

I left Inforex in 1974 and went to work for Paradyne, another company specializing in high-tech communications systems. Their specialty was producing remote printers. The work was challenging, but I was good at it. During these years I was advancing my career in these companies and making good money. I could see that if I continued on this path, I would be financially secure. Despite this success, I was still eager to strike out on my own.

PART III

Becoming a Successful Entrepreneur

Even though I had enjoyed success in the business world as an employee for several companies, I always knew my calling was to be an entrepreneur, like my father and others in our family. Owning my own business and being my own boss was a goal that seemed to have been imprinted on my DNA. As early as the 1960s I decided that I wanted to benefit from the financial opportunities available to those willing to take risks. My initial aim was to be successful in business and retire at age forty-five. I knew I would have to strike out on my own early to achieve this ambitious goal, so I began looking for ways to get into business for myself, even while I was holding down full-time jobs. In 1974 I had an equity position in a company called Community Computer Corporation that provided computer services to individuals and businesses. I knew this company would never generate significant revenue because the services it provided were not innovative; I had to turn elsewhere if I wanted to really make it big as an entrepreneur.

In 1974 I became reacquainted with Jack Dorsey, whom I had known since my days at Varian. He was an engineer in the process control automation business. With an investment of $10,000 each we began General Automotive Products. Our plan was to develop a remote-control automobile ignition device. When I lived in Minnesota, it was necessary to go outside in the cold to start the car and let it warm up —not a pleasant prospect in sub-zero weather. Often we had to place a blanket on the engine at night or disconnect the battery and bring it inside. It seemed a no-brainer that a remote starter would make life much easier for motorists in cold climates. They could start their cars remotely with the heater running, so they could step into a warm car. For the first time, I brought in an advisor, Walter Child, former Vice Chairman of Chrysler Canada's Board of Directors. I had met him three years earlier when he was CEO of an emissions company in Pennsylvania, and I now felt that General Automotive could benefit from his long-term experience in the automotive industry.

Jack Dorsey and I spent all of 1975 and most of 1976 developing and marketing our invention. If I ever needed a lesson in what can happen when one strikes out on one's own, this experience provided it. I no longer had a regular income, and my earnings from General Automotive paled in comparison to what I had earned at my previous employers. Still, the outlook in those years was promising. We managed to sell our device to several automobile dealers, until gas shortages made people more conscious of fuel costs and caused our business to dry up. Interestingly, however, we sold quite a few of these devices for installation on luxury cars that were being exported to the Middle East, where the remote starter served as a unique safety device; it could prevent the detonation of car bombs triggered when an engine was started. We introduced our product to the public in May 1976, but it never really caught on. Still, the project was not a total loss. We sold the business to the Chrysler Corporation through an intermediary, Pennfield Industries, for a decent profit.

At the end of 1976 I found employment with General Data Systems, a data processing company, where I became vice president for sales and marketing and acquired 10 percent of the equity. My responsibilities centered on sales and marketing of data process systems for claims adjustments, policy administration, and billings for insurance companies. I stayed for approximately six years but left when I found myself in the middle of a policy dispute. Eventually, General Data Systems was sold to Electronic Data Systems, a subsidiary of General Motors.

Establishing Fidelity
Investment Corporation

On May 27, 1977, while still working fulltime for General Data Systems, I started a real estate investment company called Fidelity Investment Corporation. I had studied real estate on my own and had become aware that residential real estate appreciates predominantly when inflation is higher than the prevailing interest rate. Commercial real estate appreciates based on location, the business environment, interest rates, and other inflationary factors. However, there are exceptions to this rule. The change in road networks, for example, can drive a property's value up or down. So I asked myself, "What is the best way to invest in real estate?"

It was not feasible for me to buy multiple homes and hold onto them while they appreciated in value. By doing so, I would incur all the expenses of home ownership and, in addition, be faced with the hassle of renting properties on my own. On the other hand, if I bought a large apartment building, I could hire help to take care of maintenance issues and have sufficient income to cover those expenses. However, owning an apartment building presented issues of liquidity; if I needed cash, I would have to sell the entire building. I came to the realization that the best plan was to invest in real estate that could provide some assured source of income but that could be liquidated on a short-term basis. I developed a concept that I called "builder's model

Is Lack Of Cash Holding Up America's Dream Homes?

Logo of Fidelity Investment Corporation's Builder's Model Home Purchase & Leaseback Program.

home purchase and lease back" program. The idea was to buy the model homes in builders' developments and lease them back to the builders. I would put down 20 percent and finance 80 percent. I would then lease the model home back to the builder at 12 percent per year, triple net lease, meaning the builder was responsible for all taxes, maintenance, and utilities. After closing, I would search for investors to recoup the 20 percent I had invested. In that case Fidelity Investment would become the general partner, and the investors would be limited partners, sharing part of the lease payments and gains in appreciation.

This plan offered two advantages. First, although the homes were residences, the lease-back agreements gave me the same advantage as people who own commercial real estate. The builder would have to maintain the property in order to use it as a model. He also had to make prompt lease payments, or he would be locked out of his model. Second, if I needed cash, I could sell one or more of these homes, but would not have to sell all of the units as I would with a single apartment building. I started the first program, which I designated FIC Associates I, with the purchase of six homes in Bensalem, Pennsylvania, in December 1977. Fidelity Investment was the general partner. Before too long, I had purchased homes in two other developments in southeast Pennsylvania. We exhibited at home builders' shows, and as a result, the idea was catching on throughout America. However, I was cautious, and did not want to expand beyond my ability to hold a job and work on this venture as a sideline.

Fidelity Investment experienced some success but eventually ran into problems. First, I had to deal with a copycat. About a year after I invented this program, I got a call from an official at a Savings & Loan Bank in Baltimore who wanted to go into partnership with me. He offered to provide the financing for the properties (the 80 percent required for purchase) and also put up the 20 percent down payment from the investment pools the bank managed. Somewhat naively, I fell for his pitch and, not thinking ahead, did not require him to sign a confidentiality/

nondisclosure agreement. Initially, people at the bank were very supportive. Bank officials asked many questions about the operations, visited the homes, talked with the builders involved, and attended trade shows with me. They spent time looking at my marketing techniques and reviewing my contracts. In the beginning I did not think much about their activities; I assumed they were simply trying to be a knowledgeable partner. What a shock I received when I learned that they had entered essentially the same business.

Because the bank had significant financial resources, it experienced great success early on, but eventually the hammer fell, and the program became unsustainable. I saw the handwriting on the wall and was able to bail out, but bank officials did not recognize when to get out. Additionally, in my opinion, they ignored Securities and Exchange Commission regulations and engaged in suspect business practices. Eventually the bank had to be liquidated. At the same time, as we moved into the 1980s, interest rates skyrocketed and bad loans began to pile up, resulting in a national savings and loan crisis. Although it did not help me at the time, the banker who, in my opinion, had acted so unethically was eventually ousted from his bank for taking excessive risks. He ended up going to prison for making improper loans and essentially looting his bank for personal gain. While I did not want to see anyone go to jail, I did not feel sorry for him. After all, he had profited from my hard work without giving me any compensation.

My second problem with the builder's model home purchase and lease back program arose because the residential real estate market came under heavy pressure during the late 1970s. The word on the street was that the 30-year mortgage was dead forever. What happened offers a good lesson in how outside forces over which one has no control can affect a business venture. When I began investing in model homes, the annual inflation rate in the United States was running between 4 percent and 6 percent and generally toward the lower end of this range. That meant mortgages could be obtained at reasonable rates of interest, and hence the market for new homes was robust. By the middle of the 1970s, however, inflation had begun to rise notably, climbing to 11.3 percent in 1979, followed by a staggering rise to 13.5 percent in 1980. This inflation drove up mortgage interest rates precipitously, so that by 1980 a borrower might have to pay in excess of 20 percent interest on a thirty-year mortgage—if they could get one. These circumstances made my type of real estate investment untenable, so eventually I got out of the model home market, finally terminating FIC Associates I in 1985.

Lesson Learned: *Although I made substantial money from my investments in the model home purchase and lease back program, I learned two valuable lessons:*

First, good business practices dictate that when you engage in business opportunities that require you to disclose confidential information, always have the other party sign a confidentiality/nondisclosure agreement.

Second, knowing when to exit a business is as important as knowing when to jump in. In the case of the model home venture, I realized that the business environment had turned volatile, and it was time to exit. Unlike the bank officials, I was sufficiently clued in to the housing market to recognize signs that did not bode well for the immediate future.

I kept Fidelity Investment active as a company in case market conditions changed, or in the event that I decided to purchase other properties or businesses. The decision proved wise, as I have on occasion purchased commercial properties and businesses and held them in this company. One acquisition that eventually proved highly profitable was Chadderton Airport, a private airstrip located on 117 acres in western Pennsylvania, between Sharon and Hermitage, in Hermitage Township. I bought the property on February 14, 1980, through a new limited partnership, FIC Associates XIX, with Fidelity Investment as the general partner. At this time the federal government was deregulating the airline industry. Since the Federal Aviation Administration would no longer have authority to prescribe routes to the airlines, any airline could operate out of any facility as long as it could get gates at the desired airports. It became clear that the major airlines would be operating from hubs, and smaller airports would be abandoned. I thought that it might be possible to use this airport as a feeder from Sharon to Pittsburgh where Allegheny Airlines (now US Airways) was the major carrier. To realize this vision, I needed to obtain a civil airport permit from the Pennsylvania Department of Transportation. Unfortunately, my request was denied because commercial passenger aircraft required a longer runway. Because the Chadderton airport had housing developments at both ends of the runway, there was no way to extend the landing area.

Undaunted by this setback, I turned my attention to other uses for this property, and decided to convert the airport into an office park. Two events outside my control helped me considerably in making the decision. First, the trucking industry was also deregulated, making it easier for companies to determine the best routes for getting goods across the country. At the same time, the Pennsylvania Department of Transportation completed a major upgrade of the road fronting the property, making it a major artery for truck travel. I approached officials in Hermitage Township to request rezoning. Neighbors initially opposed this development. I wanted to assure them that the new development would be an asset to the area, so I organized a town meeting at a local hotel, invited all the neighbors and the press, served light refreshments and made a visual presentation fully describing my concept and the type of tenants that would potentially locate there. The neighbors withdrew their opposition, became big supporters, and the township agreed to a zoning change. I actively sought out a tenant to erect an office building on the property on the assumption that if one business located at the park, others would follow. Eventually a doctor's office constructed a medical complex on the site. At this point the township expressed interest in the property. Beginning in 2000, officials in Hermitage began to put together a financial package to acquire the old Chadderton Airport site from me. With the assistance of the state of Pennsylvania and the federal government, the city purchased the entire remaining property, allowing me to make a handsome profit on my investment. Soon thereafter FIC Associates XIX was dissolved.

Lessons Learned: *First, it is always wise for an entrepreneur to have a vehicle available to make major investments so that these kinds of financial transactions can be separated from one's personal finances. Having a company such as Fidelity Investment Corporation allowed me to buy assets and then spin off separate companies, if the situation warranted such action.*

Second, it is not unusual for residents to oppose development in their neighborhoods because they initially have a negative reaction to such major changes. However, if they are presented with complete information and the developer proves to be a reputable individual, it is possible to turn around their opposition. Gathering facts and presenting them honestly and transparently to those who are initially skeptical of a new idea or project is the best way to transform opposition into support.

Transforming Viatek

I had known for some time that my tenure at General Data Systems was coming to an end. I had sold my stock back to the company in 1981, and I finally left the company early in 1983. "What next?" I asked myself. I still had income from various investments, including Chicago Board of Education bonds and City of Philadelphia bonds which I sold for a handsome profit that year. In fact, I was routinely supplementing my wages with income from interest and investments, so the possibility that I might be out of work was not as worrisome as it might have been earlier in my career. During the rest of 1983, when I was searching for my next new venture, my family moved about four miles from our home in King of Prussia to Wayne, Pennsylvania. Nevertheless, I knew I would have to find another business in which I might take an active role as owner or partner. I contacted a former consultant for General Automotive Products who operated a business in Bethlehem, Pennsylvania that developed radio-frequency (RF) remote-control products under the name

Viatek. Though a personable and talented engineer, he was consistently late in delivering products to his customers—sometimes years late. He seemed to operate the business "hand-to-mouth," and there was no evidence that the company would ever be on sound financial footing without implementing some serious changes in management philosophy, and instilling strong controls over operations. In 1984, after several conversations, I agreed to join the firm as executive vice president. When I arrived at Viatek, it was obvious that the company had no product focus and pursued business without a clear strategy. The company needed to focus product development on core competencies, and install rigid standards for operations and product cost control. Two years later, I bought in as an equal partner (or so I thought) and became president of the company, while my partner assumed the responsibilities of executive vice president and chief technology officer.

Within three years I turned around the business by applying sound business practices and bringing in a new board of directors, including Viatek's attorney and a retired Air Force General who could help us lobby for contracts from the government. Through my contacts in the business world, we obtained a major contract to produce air-ground communications systems for ARINC, located in Annapolis, Maryland, a co-op owned by the airlines. By 1985 we had outgrown our original facility in Bethlehem and moved into a new electronics plant in Allentown. We had plans to expand the work force to forty-five employees, and Pennsylvania's Secretary of Commerce cited us as an example of how the Lehigh Valley was on the cutting edge of the growth of high-tech industries. Clearly, Viatek was doing well, and I was able to increase salaries for both my partner and me quite handsomely. It was a productive and profitable time for the company.

Unexpectedly, in 1987 my time with Viatek came to an abrupt end, and I learned one of the most important lessons of my career. There was a problem with the way the company's shares were distributed—one that I probably knew about when I bought into Viatek, but which I chose to ignore. At the time I joined the company, my partner's family owned 6 percent of Viatek stock, and he owned the remaining 94 percent. I bought 50 percent of his shares; it seemed I was now an equal partner, but actually I owned only 47 percent of the total shares. However, after serving three years as executive vice president subordinate to my decisions as president, my partner decided he could run the company on his own. I suspect he made this move because the company now had positive cash flow, and salaries had increased substantially. He reasoned that the job would be much easier, and he could reap substantial benefits from my three years of hard-nosed management. He decided to force me out.

To understand why this coup was orchestrated, some background may be necessary. Before I joined the company, Viatek employees were accustomed to lax management, a perk that compensated for low salaries but contributed to delays in product delivery. The company's success spurred a substantial increase in salaries, and I demanded that lax management come to an end. I suspect several people did not appreciate my insistence on accountability. I did not want employees to abuse the company's resources, come and go as they wished, or use company time for personal business. In essence, I wanted to change the corporate culture. Additionally, I demanded the same level of accountability from the board. I requested that the attorney send regular bills—not a single, un-itemized statement at the end of the year. I told the General that if he wanted to continue receiving a monthly retainer to lobby for Viatek, I expected reports on his work so we knew with whom he was meeting and what our prospects were for new business.

The move to oust me occurred at a most inopportune time. On November 5, 1987 my mother died. She had experienced

Jack at Varanashi, India in 1988 kneeling on the ghat (platform) to place his mother's ashes in the water where the Ganga and Yamuna Rivers meet.

health problems, but her death was still unexpected. She passed away in her sleep. At this time Purnima was living in Tulsa, Oklahoma. We both travelled to New York to arrange her funeral and settle her affairs, which included working out a plan for Davinder's continued care. Consequently, I was away from Viatek long enough for my partner to orchestrate his takeover.

When I returned after my mother's funeral, I received a call from my partner to meet at the office that evening. When I arrived, he and the Air Force General greeted me, and led me to the conference room. I immediately recognized that something was up. Without any discussion, I was informed that the board had met while I was away and decided to discharge me. No reason was given, and I was told to clean out my office and leave immediately. I was certainly shocked at this bold step and was convinced it would not bode well for the company, but I had no choice, as my partner and his family had the majority of shares. I reluctantly turned my back on Viatek.

A few days later, Linda Ruhe, Viatek's office manager and director of finance, whom I had recruited to join Viatek, and who had reported directly to me, was also terminated. I am certain her only fault was that she was closely associated with me. According to Linda, that was the reason given for her discharge. Interestingly, that was not the end of the matter. I became engaged in a series of legal actions with shareholders of the company that did not benefit either side. Within three years Viatek went bankrupt. The only ones who made out well were the lawyers.

Lessons Learned: *From my experience at Viatek I learned two valuable lessons:*

1. *If a business is to succeed, management must define its core competencies and determine its market niche, and then concentrate efforts to become a leader in that area. At the same time, management must learn to refuse new business if it does not fall within the company's core competencies. Sometimes small companies find it difficult to turn away work because they need the business. Too often they take on jobs from clients with unrealistic expectations regarding product quality, pricing, or time constraints on delivery. There is no quicker way to end up in trouble.*

2. *It is also important to have a controlling share of the company in order to carry out business operations without fear of being removed by one or more partners who might individually, or collectively, decide to take the company in a different direction. If you do not own at least 51 percent of a company, you must accept the fact that you do not control your destiny, and you can be forced to leave the company on less than acceptable terms. Of course, the chances of that happening are reduced when there are more partners; convincing six owners to take action against one owner is much harder than getting one or two owners to go along with a plan to change management and force out a partner. On the other hand, managing a company with multiple owners presents other problems where each owner thinks he has the "best solution." Can you imagine successfully managing your company by committee? Remember the old saying that a camel is a horse designed by a committee. Lastly, I learned that if you do not own a majority share, it is important to have a written agreement from other owners that you will be bought out at a fair price if the others determine that your services are no longer needed.*

Creating Fidelity Technologies Corporation

I did not dwell on the unfair treatment I received at Viatek, but instead began immediately looking for new opportunities. I first entered into an agreement to purchase Pennfield Industries, the company to whom I had sold General Automotive Products, but the deal fell through, and I turned my attention elsewhere. Within weeks after my discharge from Viatek I learned that United Chem-Con (UCC), a company in Lancaster, Pennsylvania, had recently declared bankruptcy and was in the process of liquidating its assets. The company's decline into bankruptcy afforded me the opportunity to obtain its assets at a bargain-basement price; conversely, later legal actions taken against UCC's officials proved detrimental to my ability to create a new business using the purchased assets. Therefore, I think it helpful to explain in some detail how UCC, a company many considered a shining example of entrepreneurship and initiative only a few years earlier, ended up in bankruptcy at the end of 1987.

UCC was founded in 1978 by four investors, among them James Christian, an African American chemical engineer from Lancaster. Christian became CEO of the new company. Initially organized to manufacture photo-chemically etched circuits, by the 1980s UCC was involved in computer circuit board assembly for commercial entities such as Xerox, IBM, and DuPont. Beginning in the early 1980s, the company also began manufacturing a variety of products for use in communications systems being deployed by the U. S. Army and Navy. Because Christian was a majority shareholder, UCC qualified for "set asides" that provide small, minority-owned businesses a competitive advantage in bidding on government contracts. Under the provisions of Section 8(a) of the Small Business Act, UCC was able to obtain a number of no-bid multi-million-dollar contracts for government work.

Many of these set-asides had been arranged by Pennsylvania Congressman Joseph McDade, who was serving at that time as a ranking member of the House Appropriations Committee. Although UCC's Lancaster plant was not in McDade's Congressional District, he saw an opportunity to bring new business to the impoverished coal-country region that he represented by getting UCC to open a new plant in his congressional district and branch out beyond its core competencies in an entirely new direction: construction of large cargo containers called sea sheds for the Navy. By pulling a few strings and allegedly arranging for some payoffs disguised as political contributions and consultants' fees, McDade managed, in 1983, to secure a multi-million-dollar contract under the SBA 8(a) program for UCC to manufacture these sea sheds.

UCC opened the new plant in the town of Renovo in Clinton County, McDade's home district. The federal contracts came pouring in. The cozy arrangement allowed UCC to grow handsomely, and within three years the company had more than 450 employees at its two locations. Christian told a national magazine in 1986 that he expected the company to gross $40 million that year.

In 1987 the house of cards built by Christian and McDade collapsed. An investigation by the government led to charges against UCC for fraudulent billing. Some of its top executives and several politicians were indicted on criminal charges as well. Apparently the company had been submitting progress payment invoices claiming to have completed much more work than it had actually performed. Despite its mediocre performance, UCC had state-of-the-art facilities, including plush offices and high salaries for executives—even helicopters for their use in traveling. No doubt they had high overhead. When government funding was suspended in 1987, UCC was forced to shut down operations and declare bankruptcy.

At the time, UCC was leasing space for its operations in Lancaster. When the landlord learned of the company's bankruptcy, he immediately searched for, and found, a new tenant who needed the facility immediately. Normally UCC might have obtained a stay from eviction, but the landlord petitioned the court that he would be harmed if the company did not vacate immediately. No one challenged the petition, perhaps because UCC was in chaos; some officials were under criminal investigation and faced possible jail time for their actions, and most were worried about saving themselves. UCC was given seven days to vacate the building.

A short-notice auction was planned for December 29, 1987 to sell off the company's assets. The judge directed that sealed bids be submitted. Some buyers, interested in one or another part of the company's various operations, made low-ball bids on segments of the inventory. I did my homework quickly and made a bid through a Philadelphia attorney to the trustee designated by the bankruptcy court. The trustee was very helpful in providing information to assist me in preparing my bid. I hand-delivered my bid at the last possible moment. Through Fidelity Investment Corporation, I bid $97,000 for the entire assets that probably had a value into the millions. My bid turned out to be approximately $460.00 more than the total of all the segmented bids received. Hence, my bid allowed the trustee to sell off all the property to one buyer, saving him considerable paperwork. My bid was therefore accepted. As I learned later, I was lucky as well as shrewd in bidding for the entire assets. Another bidder had planned to make a bid for the entire assets at a figure considerably higher than I was offering, but he was late in submitting his bid, and it was rejected.

The sale stipulated that the winning bidder must take possession of the assets and remove them from the current location within three days. I had known of this provision and was aware that I could hardly meet this requirement. Therefore, before I had submitted my bid, I called the landlord and asked to rent the building for sixty days. He agreed. I knew, regardless of the stipulation in the bid documents, I now had sixty days to move my new acquisitions. Even with sixty days, I faced the daunting tasks of establishing a new company, hiring an initial management team, and relocating the huge inventory that was housed in a 100,000 square-foot building.

My first task was to quickly organize the initial management team who then could help me move the assets and establish the new company. I called Linda Ruhe, my former colleague at Viatek, and asked her to join me in my new venture. I also contacted Ron Bressler, former vice president for operations and administration at UCC, whom I had met when I was doing due diligence before purchasing UCC's assets. I thought he would be a good fit for the new operation, since he was totally familiar with the operations and administration of UCC.

Next I had to pick a name for the new company and settle on its location. Picking the name was easy as I had always liked the word "Fidelity," which means the quality of being faithful or loyal. I called the new company Fidelity Technologies Corporation. Selecting a site to house this company proved to be more difficult. Linda lived in Allentown, Ron resided in Lancaster, and I was located in Wayne. We each lived approximately fifty miles from each other. When the three of us met to make plans for the new business, we agreed to look for a facility in or near Reading, giving each of us an equal commute. We knew, too, that renting space in Reading would be less expensive than anything we would find in Wayne, Lancaster or Allentown.

Through the Industrial Development Authority in Berks County we found a facility with approximately 28,000 square feet in the old Western Electric building in Laureldale, just outside the Reading city limits. We got a great rate of $2.30 per foot for the manufacturing space and $6.00 per foot for office space, so Fidelity signed a three-year lease. Then we arranged to get the newly purchased assets moved to this new home. Despite the significant logistics involved, the move went fairly smoothly. Fidelity Technologies Corporation was incorporated in Pennsylvania on January 15, 1988, and the company opened for business in March 1988, with my initial investment of $137,000. At this time, the company had no business in hand or on the horizon. Naively, we thought we could go back to former UCC customers, but the company was so tainted by scandals that no one wanted to work with us. The three of us anticipated that during these initial months we would face difficult challenges and limited cash flow, so we all agreed to draw small salaries. We began immediately to bid on government jobs since the assets I had purchased had been used to manufacture products for the government. I had some familiarity with government procurement from my days at Univac, but had been away from the defense industry for awhile, so it was going to take us some time to get up to speed. Our strategy was to bid on contracts to produce electronic products from the government's existing blueprints and schematics. This was low-end work, with significant competition and little margins, but we had no choice; at this time we had no design capabilities. In addition, we decided to bid for field services contracts to maintain government-owned equipment located at government facilities.

In addition to Ron Bressler, I hired Dick Rosivack as Bid Proposal Manager and Paul Johnson as Coast Guard Account Manager, both also former UCC employees. Johnson landed us a small job with the Coast Guard worth approximately $60,000 to build kits for lighthouse controllers. Unfortunately, the project did not go well. We had substantially underbid the job, and a job that should have been completed in six months ended up taking eighteen months, costing us more than $370,000. Nevertheless, we finished the job, and the Coast Guard was happy with our products, so we received additional work from them.

In those early days, I was both banker and chief sales executive for Fidelity Technologies. During 1988-1989 I loaned the company money every month to cover operational expenses. Every Monday before 5:00 a.m. I drove to Washington, D.C., to call on government agencies, predominantly Navy and Coast Guard. I stayed through the end of business on Wednesday, and then drove three and a half hours home. While in Washington, I stayed at the cheapest hotel possible. I followed this grueling schedule for three years straight, and we slowly built up a project list. It looked as if we might have turned the corner.

My efforts were almost derailed, however, before we could establish our reputation in earnest. In the spring of 1989 Ron Bressler and Dick Rosivack were among seven individuals indicted by the federal government for fraud allegedly committed while they were at UCC. I was surprised, because during the period that they had worked for Fidelity Technologies, they demonstrated high character in the performance of their duties. Ron and Dick, along with four of their former colleagues, pleaded guilty and received jail sentences. In a separate proceeding, CEO James Christian was sentenced to six years in prison (later reduced to twenty-six months) and was indicted in a separate case for illegal disposal of chemical waste at the Renovo plant.

The web of corruption expanded further when, during his trial, Christian accused Lancaster businessman James Guerin, who owned 20 percent of UCC, of being the mastermind behind the fraud scheme. Guerin owned another Lancaster company called International Signal and Control (ISC), a well known, large company also involved in government contracting. ISC had hundreds of employees in Lancaster and thousands worldwide. Guerin was an icon in the Lancaster community who made significant contributions to charitable organizations and was active in local politics. He was thought to be untouchable.

Initially, no one believed Christian's accusations, but investigators eventually determined that Christian was little more than a front man for Guerin, who had masterminded a scheme to set up Christian as CEO of UCC so the company could get minority no-bid set-aside government contracts. While

Christian acted as the front man, the real management was in the hands of Guerin's henchmen, who actually managed UCC. Guerin had set up the scheme to sell ISC's obsolete inventory to UCC, thus recognizing a significant profit on inventory that really had no market value. In the meantime, UCC put this inventory on its books as assets and recorded the payables as liabilities. According to the plan, when UCC made significant profits from its no-bid minority set-aside contracts, the money went to ISC to pay for the obsolete inventory.

Had Guerin's grand scheme not unraveled, none of the fraud would have come to light. However, in 1987 Guerin sold ISC to Ferranti International, a UK firm that had been in business for over one hundred years. Ferranti had no knowledge of the fraud; Guerin had convinced Ferranti to buy ISC by creating a number of false contracts to sell arms to the Iran Contras, Iraq, Pakistan and other countries. On paper ISC looked to be extremely profitable based on legitimate sales, when actually many of the sales were either illegal or nonexistent, and there were no profits. Ferranti ended all illegal sales immediately, causing the company's cash flow to dry up. Criminal investigations in the U.S. and UK uncovered the full extent of the fraud, and the financial and legal difficulties forced Ferranti into bankruptcy in 1993. Guerin eventually received a fifteen-year prison sentence. Congressman McDade was charged with accepting more than $100,000 in illegal campaign contributions in return for steering more than $50 million in no-bid defense contracts to UCC. Although he was acquitted in 1996, the national publicity of these scandals reflected poorly on everyone associated with UCC.

The scandal turned out to have a devastating effect on Fidelity Technologies as well. Because some of our current employees ended up going to prison, many government agencies in Washington and elsewhere thought Fidelity Technologies was simply a reincarnation of UCC. Some government officials told us to our faces that their agencies would not do business with us. I suspect a significant number of our proposals were rejected solely based on our perceived association with UCC. We had to initiate a major damage control effort. I was on the road constantly for three months, visiting each one of our customers several times to show them Fidelity Technologies' total portfolio and demonstrate that we had nothing to do with UCC other than buying its assets. I pointed out that Dick Rosivack and Ron Bressler were no longer with the company, and that any wrongdoing they had been accused of was committed before joining Fidelity Technologies. Fortunately, my efforts succeeded, particularly with the Small Business Administration (SBA) and the Defense Contract Audit Agency (DCAA). This agency was especially important, because DCAA was an essential link in the approval process for obtaining government contracts. I should acknowledge, however, that initially DCAA officials were skeptical about my arguments, and I was turned down for some contracts. Eventually, however, based on contract performance and close contact with DCAA officials, they came around.

Fidelity Technologies had little business at this time, and we were behind on the Coast Guard contract for lighthouse controllers. However, the Small Business Administration was looking to expand its portfolio of companies in its minority set aside 8(a) program, so I thought we might have a chance based on my Indian nationality to get some support from the agency. I knew Fidelity Technologies was not yet eligible for such assistance, since SBA rules required a company to be in business for a minimum of two years and show success in previous contracts. However, under SBA rules the Regional

Director has authority to waive this requirement for businesses considered good candidates. I approached the Regional Director, Robert Miller, who encouraged me to apply for Section 8(a) designation as a minority-owned small business. Despite the company's current status, Miller showed confidence in Fidelity's future and approved Section 8(a) status, giving us a competitive edge in bidding on government contracts. As a result, with that advantage and a lot of hard work, by the end of 1990 we had established Fidelity Technologies as a solid company free from the unfair stigma of our association with UCC.

Lesson Learned: *Entrepreneurs must always look for the next opportunity and must not let one setback deter them from achieving their vision of owning their own companies. When I was dismissed from Viatek, it would have been easy for me to find a job working for someone else. However, that would have meant abandoning a goal I had set for myself early in my life. I also realized that, while not all partnerships are bad, I wanted to be my own boss, and launching Fidelity Technologies gave me the chance to realize that dream. Of course, the opportunity has to be right, or one can waste time and resources trying to start a business that may have no chance to succeed. At the same time, one important key to being a successful entrepreneur is the willingness to take reasonable risks and not let oneself be deterred by initial failure.*

Finding a New Home for Fidelity Technologies Corporation

By this point our three-year lease at the former Western Electric building was set to expire. In early December 1990 we asked our landlord for a lease extension. He said he would be happy to do so, but no paperwork followed. Then on December 15th, a month before the current lease was to run out, the landlord showed up at my office with a new lease—one that increased the rent by a factor of four. There was no way Fidelity Technologies could afford to pay four times our current rate. I asked him to explain the significant increase. He said he had done us a favor by granting such a low rate three years ago. The request to extend our present lease on a month-to-month basis was denied as well as my request to have a new lease on a month-to-month basis at the new rates. His directive to us was that we sign a new lease or vacate the building by January 15th, which meant we had thirty days to find a new location and move.

Clearly, I was upset that the company had to search for a new location, especially during the holiday season, and move the entire inventory in the midst of all the other responsibilities in a start-up company. Nevertheless, instead of taking the easy way out and agreeing to the new lease, I decided to meet this unexpected challenge. I immediately called the Industrial Development Authority to get information about available properties. Over the next three days, I looked at more than a dozen locations but could find nothing that met our needs at a reasonable price. Several developers were willing to build a multi-million-dollar building for Fidelity Technologies to lease, but there was no time—and the company could not afford the price anyway. Even though we did not have much business, we had a great deal of equipment and a large inventory. We were operating in less than 5,000 square feet in our current facility, but we had 22,000 square feet of space there, much of it full of equipment that we had bought from UCC and stored for future use. Items were jammed next to each other on the floor. If Fidelity Technologies were ever to make full use of this equipment, we would need twice as much space, and the company could not afford to rent 50,000 square feet of space at the prevailing rates.

The local Industrial Development Authority's executive director accompanied me to a number of sites, until he was getting tired. Then, almost as an afterthought, he showed me the old Bachman Pretzel factory on Kutztown Road, located just outside the Reading City limit. "It is not in very good shape," he said, "and it may not be what you want because it does not have high ceilings." I decided we should look at it anyway.

Bachman Pretzels was a revered name in the Reading area. The company was started in 1884 by J. S. Bachman. The McGonigle brothers had bought Bachman Pretzels in the 1930s and run it until the 1970s, when they sold out to a national food conglomerate. However, the company had ceased operating in this facility some time ago, and the building was now unoccupied. I could see there was water damage inside, indicating that there were problems with the roof. At this time, ownership was held equally by three siblings and managed as part of a trust by Meridian Bank. What made the building especially attractive to me was that it was for sale and unoccupied, meaning we could move in immediately.

I took a look around and saw that the facility could meet our needs. I asked to meet with the trustee so I could negotiate the purchase price directly with him. The trustee was asking $750,000, and I made a counter offer of $167,000. Although both the trustee and I knew it was not what the family expected, I asked him to submit my offer to the benefactors. I reminded him that the rain damage would continue and that the family would have to invest in repairs, particularly for a new roof which could cost several hundred thousand dollars. The trustee agreed, and to my surprise he allowed me to speak with the heirs directly.

As it turned out, one of the siblings had died, leaving each of his three children with one-third of his share in the building. That meant I had to deal with five people. The trustee gave me the contact information of the five heirs, three of whom lived in the Reading area and knew the deteriorating condition of the building; immediately the three signed off. I visited one of the heirs in Cape May, New Jersey—in a terrible snowstorm—and got her signature. The final person whose approval I needed lived in Buffalo, New York. I intended to visit him as well, but another snowstorm turned me back, so I telephoned and explained my situation. I agreed to send him the necessary paperwork by next-day delivery. However, when I called the next day, he said he had not signed the paperwork. My heart sank. I thought he had changed his mind, but as it turned out, UPS was unable to deliver the paperwork because Buffalo was completely snowed in. When the paperwork arrived two days later, I called to explain what had happened to cause the building to deteriorate. He was convinced that it made good business sense to sell, so he signed the paperwork and sent it back.

Armed with all the approvals I needed, I asked the trustee to arrange for quick settlement. He agreed, probably because I was a cash buyer, and with winter approaching, the building was likely to suffer even more damage. Even though this cash was needed for the operational expenses of the business, I figured it made more sense to buy the building with cash to avoid delaying settlement because we had to be out of our current location in just a few short weeks. I decided that I would get the building financed after completing the purchase. We settled on the last business day of 1990, and it took two more months to arrange financing.

Fidelity Technologies Building, Reading, Pennsylvania.

On January 2, 1991, we began to move Fidelity Technologies to its new home. I organized a team of employees and outside temporary help to transport everything from the current facility to the former Bachman Pretzel factory, a distance of approximately two miles. The team was eager to take up the challenge, offering to work nights and weekends so as not to interfere with daily business. Throughout the move the employee-in-charge and two of the temporary help were most gracious. Only later did I realize that these three had robbed me blind. High-dollar-value items such as copper pipes and solders disappeared, as well as fine china and silverware, speakers, and other electronics components. Anything that could be sold quickly had disappeared.

Even as the move was taking place, Norma Fisher, the employee responsible for dispatching the inventory from the current location and receiving the moved items at the new facility, alerted me to the thefts. She pointed out numerous items that had been stored in the old facility but had not shown up in the new building. Foolishly, I brushed her off; I could not believe that guys who were so accommodating would steal from me. However, I had to accept that the company had lost significant high value equipment during the move, but the losses paled in comparison to what we had accomplished and the opportunity to succeed that lay ahead in the new facility.

Though I had paid a pittance for the new facility, we had some major renovations to carry out. Of course, we needed a new roof immediately, but we decided we could put off some other fixes until later. We closed off sections of the building, determining to renovate them as needed and as funds became available. Our decision to complete the work piecemeal allowed us to avoid going too deeply into debt. Had we decided to renovate the entire building, Fidelity Technologies would have incurred a large debt simply to improve the building's appearance cosmetically. We decided to focus on operations, not "show and tell."

We opened for business in the new facility on January 15, 1991 and were completely out of our old premises by that date. When we went to turn in our keys, the landlord could not believe that we had actually pulled off the move. To his chagrin, his building remained unoccupied for three years. Over the next several years business at Fidelity Technologies grew steadily, and we hired many highly qualified people. Among those who eventually joined the business were my three sons. How they were integrated into the company's operations and how they eventually came to own and run Fidelity Technologies provides a good lesson for anyone wondering how to integrate the next generation into a business.

> **Lesson Learned:** *To put it simply, challenges come unexpectedly, and they must be met. It is important not to buckle under when the unexpected happens, and you think you have no choice but to accept an unpalatable solution. In my case, I could have signed the lease presented to me and continued operating my business in the current facility. Doing so, however, would likely have proven disastrous financially. It was especially challenging to find a new facility during the holiday season, but I was determined not to be pressured into making a decision that could hurt my company. The experience taught me that, when the easy choice isn't acceptable, one must look for other options. Being willing to do the hard work necessary to position one's business for success is another key to being a prosperous entrepreneur.*

Expanding Business Operations

The decade of the 1990s was a hectic but rewarding one for Fidelity Technologies. After a rocky start, we landed on our feet and business steadily increased. 1993 was a breakthrough year for the company because Fidelity landed its first contract for developing simulation equipment. Under a contract with the Department of Defense we were hired to produce the GUARDFIST II system, a computer-based forward observer simulator for training artillery units in the U.S. Army National Guard. If we fulfilled all the terms of this contract, by far the largest we had landed to date, we would realize millions in revenue. In the same year, I was honored as central Pennsylvania's Entrepreneur of the Year. While I was proud of this personal honor, my colleagues and I knew that the real honorees were the people employed at Fidelity. We received more good news that year when Inc. Magazine recognized Fidelity Technologies as #11 on the "Inc. 500" list of fastest growing privately held companies in the United States. The following year Fidelity

GUARDFIST II Computer-Based Forward Observer Simulator manufactured by Fidelity Technologies.

appeared on the list again, this time at # 227. By that time the company had two hundred employees, seventy of them in Berks County and the rest engaged in field services at military bases throughout the country. Revenues were in excess of $10 million.

In 1995 I was again selected as central Pennsylvania's Entrepreneur of the Year, and Fidelity Technologies was named the SBA Minority Manufacturing Firm of the Year. I was extremely proud to accept this award on behalf of all Fidelity employees at a national gathering in Washington, DC during Minority Enterprise Development Week. Our good fortunes were publicized in the press, and morale at Fidelity went up appreciably. We could say with justifiable pride, "Look how far we have come from those early days when it was hard to get business because of the unfair association with UCC!"

These kinds of awards and honors were important not only because they made us feel good about what we were doing, but also because they gave us great recognition among suppliers and potential customers. We began to receive inquiries from companies and government agencies wanting to do business with us. On the other hand, calls from vendors interested in selling us their products consumed considerable time, but on the whole, the publicity was beneficial.

Once Fidelity Technologies was firmly established, I became concerned that our work was 100 percent in government contracts, so I started to look for opportunities to diversify. I investigated working in the commercial market but found Fidelity Technologies could not be successful; our manufacturing standards were too stringent for that market and our prices too high. Of course, we were proud that we could manufacture products to military specifications, or "Mil-Spec," but it proved to be a drawback when we tried to compete for commercial business. Ironically, today the government has adopted the ISO 9000 standard for its products, having abandoned the higher "Mil-Spec" standards in all but a few areas.

Since going into the commercial market was not likely to prove profitable, we looked elsewhere to expand our operations. I asked our accountants, Ernst & Young, to help us identify a business in which we might be successful. They recommended security systems. We thought that idea had promise, but I soon discovered that this business required substantial capital up front. Most companies in the industry installed systems for free or at greatly reduced rates, and offered incentives like free upgrades. That meant there was no income to offset the capital expense of manufacturing the systems or the labor costs for installation and sales. The money was made by receiving monthly payments on multi-year contracts. We did not have the capital reserves to implement this strategy. We also investigated going public and bringing in new investors. However, my experience with Viatek had convinced me that I did not want to be partners with anyone.

Instead, diversification occurred as a result of a number of acquisitions. In 1992 I began expanding our business in technology companies with the purchase of FDL Technology in Duluth, Minnesota. Unlike Fidelity Technologies that depended on the military for its work, FDL specialized in the assembly of electronics components for civilian government agencies, principally the Federal Aviation Administration (FAA). FDL had been created under Section 8(a) by the Fond du Lac Indian Tribe, whose reservation is located just fifteen miles west of Duluth. The company was not doing well, and I was approached by a major shareholder to see if I would be interested in buying the company. I investigated the opportunity and determined that there might be some promise, and also figured that, if the company could not be sustained in its present location, I could eventually merge it with Fidelity Technologies. I decided I would try to manage the company myself and spent considerable time between 1992 and 1994 shuttling back and forth between Pennsylvania and Minnesota—including some harrowing trips in the dead of winter—but eventually decided to merge the company with Fidelity.

My first venture overseas occurred in 1992 as well. Through an intermediary I was made aware of a Swiss company, Cossonay Cable SA, which had recently been purchased by Alcatel, an international conglomerate headquartered in France. Alcatel was in the process of shedding companies that were not related directly to its core competencies. Alcatel executives had assigned Cortaillod SA, a Swiss company it also owned, to manage Cossonay's operations and arrange to sell off those parts of the company that did not support Alcatel's core business strategies. Among these was a division called Cossonay Meteorology. This division manufactured anemometers, devices used to measure wind speed, direction, and temperature. A large U.S. company initially had agreed to buy Cossonay Meteorology, but when the deal fell through, an intermediary introduced me to Claude Romy, an executive with Cortaillod. I expressed to Romy my interest in purchasing the division and eventually met with him in Switzerland. After some negotiations I agreed to the purchase, and we completed the transaction in late 1992. I hired local management, so that I would have someone on site that knew the local business culture and was familiar with regulations for doing business in Switzerland.

Anemometers manufactured by Cossonay Meteorology System in Lausanne, Switzerland.

On my return trip from Switzerland I read Cortaillod's annual report and saw that among its holdings was Telectronic SA, a company that produced alarm transmission systems and Personal Emergency Response Systems (PERS) under the name TeleAlarm, for the Swiss marketplace. While the company at that time was devoting more attention to its alarm transmissions systems, I was most interested in PERS, because I thought there was greater potential for this system in the future. I wrote to Jean-Claude Vagnières, CEO of Cortaillod Group, to ask if he were willing to sell me Telectronic SA. He said he would consider such a sale but would have to seek offers from others so he could determine the division's market value. However, he encouraged me to work with Claude Romy with whom I had already worked successfully to purchase Cossonay Meteorology. After the bidding process was over, I was able to complete the purchase of Telectronic SA in August 1993. I needed to raise 3.25 million Swiss francs (CHF), approximately $2.9

Personal Emergency Response System manufactured by TeleAlarm Group in Switzerland, 2005. *(Photo by TeleAlarm Group)*

million, to purchase shares, reimburse shareholders' accounts, recapitalize the company, and cover research and development costs. I contributed $1 million CHF. With the help of Frederic Geissbuhler, a partner at my Swiss accounting firm, Price

Waterhouse Cooper (PWC), I was able to organize a bank loan for 1.5 million CHF, of which 500,000 CHF was guaranteed by the government of Canton Neuchatel, and an additional direct loan and job creation credits from the Canton Neuchatel for 750,000 CHF. At the time Telectronic had assets of 5.7 million CHF and liabilities of 3.5 million CHF, but had been unprofitable for several years. The experience taught me that one can succeed handsomely by dealing fairly with people, so that both parties achieve their mutual goals.

Two years after the purchase, by implementing my business vision, Telectronic had prospered and was ready for international expansion. Shortly thereafter, however, I learned another valuable lesson about dealing with unscrupulous executives who wish to profit from the investment and hard work of others. In Switzerland at this time the laws required that the majority of the directors of a company be Swiss nationals. Consequently, I retained one of the previous directors of the company who had helped me arrange the bank loan. Out of the blue, this director demanded that I sell the company to him. At the time of my purchase he also had an interest in purchasing Telectronic, but because he was an employee of Cortaillod and also a board member of Telectronic, he had a conflict of interest. But now, two years later, he had left Cortaillod and wanted to strike out on his own. He decided to force me to either sell to him or suffer serious financial consequences. He pointed out that he had connections with the bank and threatened to contact his friend, the bank president, to have him call in my loan. As a board member he knew I could not afford to pay off the loan immediately and would be forced to liquidate or sell the company to him.

Clearly, I took the threat very seriously. Here I was, three thousand miles away in the U.S., being caught in a squeeze play. I gave some thought to bringing this gentleman into the company in some way, perhaps as a partner or a shareholder, but I had serious misgivings about any such arrangement. So I contacted Frederic Geissbuhler at Price Waterhouse, who had helped me arrange the bank loan and knew the bank president as well. Geissbuhler organized a meeting for me with the bank president during which I explained my situation. The bank assured me that it would not recall the loan. Knowing that the bank would back me up, I immediately fired the director from the board.

I do not want to suggest that everything went smoothly in this new overseas venture. We decided to phase out the alarm transmission system business, gradually diminishing our efforts in that area and eventually selling off that product line. More immediately, however, we focused on putting into place good management practices. As a result, the business was doing well, and it became clear that we would be in Switzerland for many years to come. At that time, we were renting the Telectronic facility. In order to avoid the situation that I had experienced at Fidelity Technologies, where our rent could have sharply increased, I became interested in purchasing the building. At that time foreigners could not purchase property in Switzerland without first obtaining government approval. In 1995, after much difficulty I was granted permission to purchase the Telectronic building. In preparation for the purchase, I had formed a new company in Switzerland, Fidelity Investment Corporation – Swiss Branch, which negotiated the buy and sell agreement with Cortaillod and finalized the purchase.

The next year, in our haste to expand internationally, and without significant planning or allocation of sufficient resources, we decided to establish Telectronic GmbH in Germany under the management of the Swiss general manager. At the same time we

TeleAlarm SA building in La-Chaux-de-Fonds, Switzerland.

formed Gulati and Co. as the holding company for our Swiss and German operations. The same year we established Telectronic Corporation in the United States, under my supervision. Telectronic SA spent more than 1 million CHF to hire staff and set up an office in Germany. Unfortunately, this initiative did not produce profitable results because our present product was not adapted to all the technical standards required throughout Germany. Additionally, the country was simply too large to be covered adequately by one representative and a secretary; there was no way a single individual could market and service the product in such a large country. Eventually, we terminated German operations and liquidated the company. The Telectronic Corporation in the United States, having no more significant resources than the German company, suffered similar results. These ventures cost my companies 1.5 million CHF. Telectronic Corporation in the U.S.

changed its name to TeleAlarm, then became Fidelity TeleAlarm when I formed the international Fidelity Group (discussed later), then became TeleAlarm again when I sold Fidelity Technologies Corporation. Finally, it was merged into another one of my companies, SafetyCare Technologies.

Lessons Learned: *My experience with Telectronic SA and succeeding ventures provide several valuable lessons:*

First, I learned that it is important, when buying a new company, to analyze its operations carefully and develop a strategy for focusing on those product lines that will be profitable over a long period, and jettisoning those that will not. In the case of Telectronic SA, I concentrated on developing the personal emergency response line and gradually reduced the resources put into the alarm transmission systems product line. It is important to concentrate resources on the product or products that offer the greatest potential for success.

Second, my attempts to expand Telectronic too quickly exposed one of my weaknesses. I jumped into this venture without fully understanding the market. My experience in this endeavor taught me a valuable lesson: You must have the right product in the right market that is adapted to the culture and standards of the country. Developing a keen sense of what will work in the environment in which a business is to operate is critical if one is to achieve long-term results in any venture.

At one point during the mid-1990s, I was running nine companies: Fidelity Technologies Corporation, Telectronic Corporation SA (Swiss), Fidelity Investment Corporation,

FIC Associates XIX, Cossonay Meteorology Systems SA (Switzerland), Cossonay Meteorology Systems Inc. (U.S.), Telectronic Corporation (U.S.), Telectronic GmbH (Germany) and Gulati & Co. Devoting appropriate time and attention to each was becoming a challenge. I realized I did not have sufficient expertise or time to supervise all aspects of the growing companies and also do strategic planning. If I were to pay attention to strategy and growth, I needed someone else to handle day-to-day operations at Fidelity. In concert with my philosophy of promoting from within whenever possible, I considered two candidates for this position: Linda Ruhe, who had been with me at Viatek and at the start of Fidelity in 1988, and my marketing director, Al Jodzio, who had joined Fidelity in 1991. After considerable internal deliberations, in June 1994 I promoted Jodzio to Chief Operating Officer and Senior Vice President. Linda Ruhe decided to leave Fidelity Technologies in March 1995. In December 1995 Al Jodzio was promoted to President of Fidelity Technologies. Within a year I realized that Al Jodzio was more valuable to the company in his original position as marketing director, so I reassigned him as Vice President of Marketing and re-assumed the presidency myself. Eventually, Al Jodzio; Paul Johnson, our Coast Guard connection; and Dick Rosivack, who had returned to Fidelity after serving his prison sentence, left to form their own company. Jodzio became its president. Their new firm got most of its initial business from customers with whom they had established relationships while at Fidelity.

Soon after the trio had left, Jodzio's wife called to tell me that Al had suffered a major heart attack, and she sounded distraught because Al's new company did not provide health insurance. I assured her that, because Al had left Fidelity in a professional manner and only very recently, he was still on our policy and could be covered for his illness. I also immediately reinstated him as an employee at Fidelity so his coverage would continue. He recovered in six or seven months, and while he was recuperating, we made sure he received full benefits. When he was well, instead of rejoining Johnson and Rosivack, he returned to Fidelity as Vice President of Marketing and remained until his retirement in 2011. Sometime later, Rosivack also returned to Fidelity as a consultant.

Lesson Learned: *My dealings with Al Jodzio illustrate a principle I have employed in all my businesses: Treat employees like family and they will, in the majority of cases, remain loyal and productive. Certainly there will always be a few rotten apples; however, these instances should not deter you from treating all associates fairly. Over the long term, a cadre of loyal employees can be one of the most valuable assets in any business. Keeping good employees is important in holding down costs as well. There will be less need to spend money and time to recruit and train replacements, and long-time employees often develop a sense of "investment" in the companies for which they work.*

Forming an Advisory Board

In 1995 I set to work forming an advisory board to help with long-range planning. I envisioned a five-member board (plus myself) that would bring expertise in the fields of government, military, security, and Swiss business. Sometime earlier I had met Edwin Meese III, the 75th U.S. Attorney General under President Ronald Reagan. He currently held the Ronald Regan Chair in Public Policy at the Heritage Foundation, and was a distinguished visiting fellow at the Hoover Institute at Stanford University. I was reintroduced to him at a political fundraiser in Wayne, Pennsylvania, and I asked if he would have any interest in serving on a board at a small electronics company. He was intrigued and agreed to come to Reading to see our operations. He made the trip and liked what he saw. "I'll join you," he said. Years later, I asked why he had joined, especially since the remuneration was not a major incentive. He said that he had been in government or the legal profession for most of his life, and joining our board allowed him to make a substantial contribution to an industrial company that had a bright future. Landing a figure of Meese's stature as the first advisory board member was a real coup.

As soon as Meese joined the board, I mentioned to him that we needed a military person to advise us, since much of our work was being done for the military. He made several suggestions, among them General John W. Vessey, Jr., who had served two-terms as Chairman of the Joint Chiefs of Staff during President Reagan's administration. His military career spanned forty-six years, having started as a private in the Minnesota National Guard. Meese contacted General Vessey to ascertain his interest. Vessey requested our business plan, which we sent to him immediately, but I warned him that our plan was 200 pages long. He seemed unphased. I realized then that people in his position are accustomed to receiving large documents that they must digest in a short time.

General Vessey came to Reading, and we put on a show for him—as much as we could anyway, considering our building dated from the 1950s. The general noticed fresh paint in the building and asked if we had done that because he was coming. I admitted that we had. As we walked through the production area, Vessey stopped to talk to some employees on the assembly line. He asked one young lady if she liked working at Fidelity Technologies. She seemed very nervous but told him that she really liked working here. He asked why she liked her job. She replied that she felt she was part of a family, receiving a reasonable wage from people who cared about her.

At the end of his visit General Vessey agreed to join our board. Years later, I asked him, as I had Ed Meese, why he had accepted a position on the board. He said there were two reasons. "First, remember when I asked about the paint and you said you had done it because I was coming? I respect that kind of honesty; it is a small thing, but it helps one get a sense of the whole person. Second, when I heard from one of the employees that she felt she was working in a family environment, I thought: This is a family business, it looks as if it could do well, and I could help."

General Vessey's observations about my honest answer to his question concerning the paint job reminded me of an old wives' tale my mother used to tell us children about a boy who started stealing small items and bringing them home. His mother encouraged his stealing; she was happy that he was bringing useful items. So he kept stealing, bigger and bigger items, and his mother kept giving her blessing. When he was finally caught and came before the judge to be sentenced, he turned around and bit off his mother's ear. The judge asked why he did this. The man replied that his mother had given a sympathetic ear to his thievery; had she not done so, he most likely would have stopped. The same is true when you tell a small lie; it tends to grow, and eventually you will be caught in a bigger lie.

With Attorney General Meese and General Vessey on board, I next invited Claude Romy to join us because of his European, and specifically Swiss, business and cultural expertise. Claude was a Swiss Certified Public Accountant and an experienced executive in finance and management as well as mergers and acquisitions for multi-national companies. In addition to English, he spoke French, German, and Italian. Lastly, I invited Joseph P. Freeman, whom I had met at a security industry conference where I was exhibiting Telectronic products. Joe was a well-known consultant and publisher of market studies for the security and automation industries. He was also serving on the Board of Directors of the Security Industry Association and the Home Automation Association.

The Board's stellar credentials and their ability to contribute sound advice became increasingly important as Fidelity

Board of Advisors, wearing TeleAlarm caps, at dinner in La-Chaux-de-Fonds, Switzerland in 1996. Standing *(left to right)*, Joseph P. Freeman, Lucille Freeman, Ursula Meese, Attorney General Edwin Meese III, unidentified guest, Rosemary Gulati. Seated *(left to right)* Avis Vessey, General Jack Vessey, Claude Romy.

Technologies and Telectronic expanded into worldwide operations. The board was set up to function in an advisory capacity. They owned no stock in the company and were not highly paid; however, they did receive compensation in the form of per diem and expenses. The advantage of this arrangement for them was that, as advisors rather than directors, they incurred no liability for their participation. On the other hand, I was not bound to accept their counsel. In most instances I listened to the board's advice with appreciation. However, in some important issues, when I ignored their advice, it proved unwise.

The Board proved to be a dynamic group. In 1997 Telectronic had decided to exit the security business and enter the newly-emerging telemedicine industry, so Joe Freeman resigned. A year later Claude Romy resigned, and we were fortunate to find William W. Chorske, a replacement of exceptional caliber. Jack Vessey recommended him, and he turned out to be a real barn-burner in the board room. Chorske had recently retired as Chairman of LifeRate Systems. Previously, he had served as President of Medtronic Europe, headquartered in Switzerland, and as Senior Vice President and Chief Financial Officer of Medtronic, Inc., headquartered in Minnesota. This company specialized in implantable and interventional therapies. Vessey approached Chorske to determine his interest in joining us. He came for a visit to see if he filled a need on the board, and to allow the board to decide if he was a good choice. We all agreed, and Chorske accepted the appointment.

> **Lesson Learned:** *My only regret in creating my advisory board is that I did not do so earlier. Every owner should create an advisory board as soon as possible after a business is up and running. Even the smallest business can profit from having advisors. People like to help others, so long as they feel the owner is sincere in seeking their advice and not simply exploiting them. Advisors should not be appointed just because they engage in business with the company or because the owner expects the board member to solicit business for the company. The advisor's only role is to provide counsel on long-term strategy and broad management issues.*
>
> *The board does not have to be large, and the procedures for selecting board members and gathering their opinions and*

advice need not be elaborate. One can assemble an effective advisory board by finding three to five people who can provide advice on various aspects of the business: marketing, finance, technology, communications, or government relations, for example. Building a board with specific expertise can serve a company and its owner(s) well in the long run. On the other hand, inviting friends to sit on the board is not usually a good idea. Having friends on your board can be comforting, but it is important to remember: advisors should be able to give honest counsel, even when it is hard for an owner to hear. Unless your friends have the expertise you need and the ability to speak frankly about tough business matters, you will do better to look elsewhere for the people who can really help you.

To create a board from scratch, it is helpful to consider skill sets rather than specific people. Determine what expertise would be an asset to have on the board, and then use that matrix to seek out individuals who bring those skills. You might, for example, feel that a lawyer would make an important contribution. Once that has been determined, your search can become more focused. Certainly, personality should also enter into your process. If someone is not a good fit, he or she will not be effective. However, personality should be considered only after a candidate with the proper skills has been identified for consideration.

Learning the Hard Way about Management Team Skills

In 1999, the owners of the British manufacturer Tunstall, the largest company in the personal security industry, indicated a desire to sell the company. We were invited to submit an offer. At the time, Tunstall had annual revenues of £160 million. Although their size was significantly larger than Telectronic, we thought we had a shot at acquiring them. We investigated the company and made some initial contacts. Through a mergers & acquisitions specialist at Price Waterhouse UK, we were put in touch with Mercury Private Equity, then a division of Merrill Lynch, a group that could provide the funding we would need for the purchase. We submitted our bid and were selected as potential purchasers. We felt Tunstall did not have the management in place to run the company effectively, so we decided to bring in our management teams from Reading and Switzerland to meet with Mercury to finalize a post-acquisition business plan. Frankly, our Reading team did not make a good impression. In fact, after the meeting Mercury decided to pursue the deal alone and retain Tunstall's existing management team.

Of course, we were disappointed because we had made all the right arrangements with Mercury, and they had committed to financing the acquisition for us before changing their minds and purchasing the company themselves. Our legal advisors in both the U.S. and the UK thought that we had strong grounds for legal action, but after discussing the matter with my board of advisors, we decided not to do so since I knew such a suit would take years to settle. Additionally, any legal action would most likely have to be brought against the company in England, where the loser pays all court costs. I did not want to put my company in such a risky position.

> **Lesson Learned:** *We tried to make a big leap—and failed. This was a bitter pill for me to swallow. I discovered that I would have to improve my senior management team if we were ever going to take a leading role on the world business stage. My vision at this time was to create a global company, but I did not pay sufficient attention to having world-class management in place. I thought I could buy companies like Tunstall and then put the right people in place. I learned that one has to plan and be ready when the opportunity comes to move into a larger market.*

At this time my global vision was to consider further diversification and increase our research and development and management teams, so I was delighted when, in 1999, Telectronic SA was approached by CSEM (Centre Suisse d' Electronique et de Microtechnique), a research and development think tank located in Switzerland. That company was partially funded by the Swiss federal government for the purpose of developing new technologies for industrial use. Industrial partners for whom they developed projects provided the remainder of the funding. CSEM had completed a feasibility study for the development of a project called CosyMed, an innovative plan to create telemedicine for people living independently. CSEM approached Telectronic to be a partner in this venture. This overture was my introduction to providing medical services for people living at home. The idea was to combine vital signs monitoring with our Personal Emergency Response System (PERS).

To advise us on this innovative project, we brought in a new Board member, John C. Beck, M.D., whose name appeared frequently in medical journals as an expert on geriatric care. Also, he had participated in the CSEM feasibility study. He was a professor at the multi-campus Program in Geriatric Medicine and Gerontology at the UCLA School of Medicine, and was past chair of the Department of Medicine at McGill University in Montreal. Ed Meese contacted Dr. Beck, who expressed some interest in joining the Board of Advisors at Fidelity Group. I met with him in California, and after some conversation he agreed to join us.

I calculated that the project would cost 5 million CHF, and we decided to proceed. The Swiss government provided 1.3 million CHF toward the cost of the project, and Telectronic financed the rest. Initially the project showed promise, but while CSEM proved to be an excellent partner regarding research and development, it had difficulty developing production units. After some initial success, we never realized the full potential of this idea.

Personal and Family Matters

One of the difficulties in writing the story of one's business career is that events seem to take place in isolation from everything else going on in one's life. However, during the decades when I was establishing myself as an entrepreneur, and especially while I was building Fidelity Technologies into a first-rate firm and expanding my holdings overseas, I continued to be involved with my family and my community. My activities as a father and civic leader are described in some detail in Part IV of this book. It seems appropriate at this point, however, to mention what happened to my brother, Davinder, whose care occupied us, but especially Rosemary, for nearly a decade.

For twenty years after my father died, my mother and brother managed to accommodate themselves to life in the apartment in New York City. My mother grew to enjoy walking through the neighborhood, tending to her window garden, and socializing with friends in the apartment building, particularly a retired ballet dancer and a nurse who worked in a physician's office on the first floor. My mother received her medical care from that physician, and the stores where she shopped were located within a few blocks of the building, so she managed fairly well without the need of a car or too much reliance on public transportation.

Davinder, after moving to Pennsylvania, in front of Christmas tree in 1989.

Despite his mental illness, Davinder was able to shop, cook, take the bus to the doctor's office, and help my mother with household chores. In turn, she saw to his needs and made certain he received appropriate medical attention. The two lived together in that apartment until November 1987, when my mother died. Davinder did not want to relocate, and we did not force him to move immediately. Davinder remained in New York for a few months, until we could make arrangements to bring him to Pennsylvania to live near us. After much searching we were able to purchase a condominium nearby. Rosemary provided complete care for him, including doctors' visits, shopping, household chores, and making sure he had his medicines. Davinder enjoyed being on his own. He walked to a nearby shopping center and around the neighborhood. However, over the ten-year period we looked after him, he gradually showed signs of deterioration. He suffered from high blood pressure, high cholesterol, and diabetes. Medicines prescribed to treat these ailments counteracted the drugs he was taking for his psychological illness. Eventually, he was forced to make radical changes in his diet, but nothing we or his physicians did seemed to improve his health; over time he went downhill and gradually lost the ability to live on his own. We were advised by Social Services to find him a place where he could be cared for professionally. This was no easy task. Nursing homes where he could receive treatment for his physical ailments were not equipped to deal with his psychological disability, and facilities designed to deal with psychological problems did not have the ability to treat his physical conditions. Finally, we found a personal care home in Lansdale that agreed to take him. Rosemary visited him weekly, and we were pleased with the care he received. Unfortunately, he died of complications from diabetes at the early age of fifty-three on August 1, 1998.

Managing a Worldwide Enterprise

Most of the companies I acquired were struggling when I bought them. That's why I was able to obtain them at good prices. I was required to spend considerable time on-site until I could be assured that managers were capable of running these companies in a manner that met my expectations. Managing companies in the United States and Switzerland proved to be a demanding task. I worked in Switzerland for two weeks and then returned to the U.S. to work at Fidelity for two weeks. I again headed back to Switzerland for a week, and returned to the United States to spend three weeks at Fidelity, and then repeated the pattern. The pace was grueling, but I felt I had to be on the spot in both places to provide hands-on leadership.

To make management more complicated, when Telectronic was originally started, the founding partners lived in different cities. Consequently, the company's corporate headquarters and research and development arms were based in Geneva, while the manufacturing, customer support, and financial services operations were located in La-Chaux-de-Fonds, necessitating an hour and a half train ride plus a half-hour walk to travel between locations. When the Board of Advisors first visited these facilities in 1996, they recommended that all operations be consolidated in La-Chaux-de-Fonds. Peider Pinosch, Telectronic's General Manager, insisted that this consolidation was not possible. People in Switzerland did not relocate, and if we chose to move the Geneva operations, we would lose our research and development talent. He hired an outside consulting firm to support his position. After months of fruitless effort to convince him otherwise, I made the decision in favor of consolidation at La-Chaux-de-Fonds. Pinosch was not happy, as he lived in Geneva and would now be forced to endure a long commute, but to his credit, he did the best job he could under the circumstances. Only Director of Engineering Pierre-Alain Nicati and Chief Digital Engineer Tibor Ganyi, both key positions, chose to relocate. Under the leadership of Nicati and Ganyi, the remainder of the engineering staff was replaced. Though this task was not easy, in the end our new staff had better competencies.

On the negative side, because of his extensive commute time, Peider Pinosch came to La-Chaux-de-Fonds only two or three days each week, and the performance of the company suffered as a result. On the advice of my Board of Advisors, I decided to replace Pinosch. Nicati was appointed General Manager and Ganyi became Director of Engineering and Production. This move proved most advantageous; these two formed one of the best management teams with whom I had ever worked. Nicati remained with the company until it was sold to Bosch in 2006 and stayed with Bosch for approximately two years after the transfer of ownership. Ganyi stayed with the company until 2005, when he married and moved to the north of Switzerland.

Lessons Learned: *You should make decisions regarding whether to move a company location, shift from one product line to another, or realign resources based on an analysis of business needs. In this context, it is important to listen to your management team and consider their recommendations carefully and dispassionately. At the same time, you must insure that the management team does not make recommendations about proposed changes based on their personal preferences. Anyone can come up with reasons why something should not be done. The entrepreneur/owner must recognize that the objections people raise are obstacles that must be overcome; it is important to treat these objections fairly and directly.*

Once you have made a decision, you must communicate it in no uncertain terms, explaining what you want done and when tasks must be accomplished. You must set a firm deadline for carrying out your decision. At the same time, you must take into account the local culture. That advice applies no matter where your company is located. People who are asked to move or to abandon a product line are likely to express initial skepticism or downright opposition, whether they live overseas or in the United States. For many, any change is hard, but as the owner, you must act in the best interests of your business.

Business continued to grow with the strong management team in place. In 2001 I became interested in Antenna AB; a bankrupt Swedish company that made products similar to those manufactured by Telectronic in Switzerland. Antenna had a much broader distribution network, with wholly-owned subsidiaries in Sweden, Germany, the United Kingdom, Hong Kong, and the Netherlands. I worked with the bankruptcy administrator to develop a bid to purchase the company and managed to submit the winning bid of $1 million. Integrating the two companies presented a challenge, but Pierre-Alain Nicati in Switzerland handled this assignment expertly.

In 2001 I formed Fidelity Group as a means of bringing together my various companies under a single corporate entity. The international Fidelity Group consisted of Fidelity Technologies Corporation and the newly formed TeleAlarm Group, an umbrella organization consisting of Telectronic SA (Switzerland), Fidelity TeleAlarm (United States), Antenna TeleAlarm AB (Sweden), Antenna Care UK (England), TeleAlarm GmbH (Germany), Antenna Care BeNeLux B.V. (Netherlands), and Antenna Care Asia Ltd. (Hong Kong). Fidelity Investment (U.S. and Switzerland) and JDG Holding SA (Switzerland) were also part of Fidelity Group.

Then I made one of the biggest mistakes of my career. The TeleAlarm Group in Europe had more than tripled in size. Fidelity Technologies and my other related enterprises in the United States were doing quite well and growing rapidly. I simply could not continue to travel back and forth as I had been doing for the past nine years. The newly-formed Fidelity Group needed experienced senior-level management; however, my first attempt to hire such management was not successful.

Sometime earlier I had met the Chief Executive Officer of a Midwest company involved in manufacturing various electronics products in the healthcare industry. I set up a meeting with him to explore his interest in working with me at Fidelity Group. He treated me very graciously during our day-long interview, and my initial impression was positive. I asked if he might like to join us in Reading, and he was open to the idea. He was originally from the Philadelphia area, so the move would be a kind of homecoming for him. I told him I would take his resume to my board to get their opinion before making a formal offer.

The board looked at the resume and said they thought that I could find a more suitable candidate. I understood the reasons for their opinion, but I was insistent and pressed them to meet my candidate at the next Board meeting. They conceded, and when the next meeting convened in Reading, they met with my selection for nearly an hour. Afterwards, Jack Vessey led the board's discussion. He made it clear that he thought this candidate was not the best choice to be my second in command. Both Bill Chorske and Ed Meese also encouraged me to continue the search.

I chose to ignore the board's advice, and I hired my candidate anyway. I reasoned that I was now overburdened trying to manage a far-flung conglomerate on my own. I had a company in Sweden with branches all over the world, a company in Switzerland with a branch office in the United States, and Fidelity Technologies. I offered my candidate the job as CEO of TeleAlarm Group at a handsome salary with generous bonuses.

I had hired my new CEO with the expectation that initially he would manage day-to-day operations of the seven companies under the TeleAlarm Group. I could then concentrate my energies on Fidelity Technologies, which was at this time also expanding rapidly into the international marketplace. There was a possibility that, eventually, he would also take over the management of Fidelity Technologies. My relationship with the CEO started out well. He was helpful almost immediately in the acquisition of Avalon Healthcare Solutions, a software package designed to enhance emergency communications in the senior housing industry. I thought I had made a good choice.

Before long, however, I began to question my decision. Within a few months, the new Chief Executive had supplemented the management team in the U.S. and Europe with his former associates. He did so without sufficient consideration of how the additional staff would contribute to increased revenues and profitability, and within four months, the TeleAlarm Group had added nearly $1 million in overhead. It became obvious that he did not have an understanding of the financial side of the business. To provide him with additional support in the financial area, I brought in a new Chief Financial Officer (CFO) for Fidelity Group. Our bankers introduced me to a candidate who seemed to have the requisite credentials, and I agreed to hire him at a substantial salary with bonuses. He was to report to me, but work alongside the new CEO.

After several months with the new company hierarchy, I became increasingly disenchanted with my CEO. He was required to report quarterly to the board, which he did fairly well in the beginning. Despite their original misgivings, the board provided him all the support and guidance his position required. Eventually, however, the board began to express some reservations about his leadership, especially since the TeleAlarm Group's objectives were not being met. Then, one of his former associates, whom he had hired as General Manager of Fidelity TeleAlarm, resigned without notice. This resignation bothered me. It is not unusual in business for a chief executive to bring in his own team. Executives depend on these loyal and proven subordinates to improve business operations. Hence, the abrupt resignation of a key team member gave me a strong indication that the employees on my CEO's team were not as devoted to him as one might have thought.

After the new CEO had been with the company a year, I finally decided that the board had been right; he was not a good fit for us and had to go. Unfortunately, that meant I was again forced to take over daily operations of all the companies within the Fidelity Group. By this time our European operations were eating up a lot of cash, and Fidelity Technologies was serving as the "sugar daddy" supporting the overseas operations. We eventually ended up doing a major financial write-off to get Fidelity Technologies and the European companies back on track.

To make my predicament worse, my new CFO also was not working out as I had anticipated, mainly because he did not understand the culture of our company. Among his first actions when he arrived, despite the fact that he had an appropriately furnished office, was to order brand-new office furniture. I was concerned because we typically purchased "nearly new" furniture. When I questioned him on his decision, he responded that he never uses someone else's furniture; wherever he goes, he buys new furniture. I let the matter slide since the CFO had been with us only a few weeks. However, he was to disappoint me on much more important matters as well. In 2001, I became interested in acquiring ECC International Corporation, a publicly traded company in Orlando, Florida. The company manufactured simulators and trainers for the military and served the same market as Fidelity Technologies. I assigned the CFO to be the point man for this acquisition. We and our investment banker flew to Orlando to perform due diligence. At our meeting with ECC executives, the CFO contributed little to our discussions. He did develop a long list of items that he suggested we investigate. When I looked at the list, I saw that about 80 percent of the items were irrelevant for our business. The issues were more appropriate for vetting call centers, the industry in which he had worked before joining Fidelity Group. Clearly I was disappointed, not only in this instance but also in his failure to develop creative financing and operational business options. This potential acquisition went nowhere, since we could not agree on price. I allowed the CFO to remain at the company for the next nine months, but eventually decided it was in the company's best interest if we parted ways.

Lessons Learned: *My experience in hiring these new executives taught me several valuable lessons:*

First, while a business owner is not obligated to follow all recommendations of an advisory board, it is of utmost importance to defer to the board on important matters. It is clear that I should have listened to my advisors who were unanimous in recommending against hiring the person I had selected as CEO.

Second, it is essential that any candidate under serious consideration be fully vetted. In my rush to get someone in the job, I sacrificed my own management principles to expediency.

Third, it is important to conduct a thorough search to find the best candidates for all positions, but especially for executive-level positions; one cannot simply limit the search to one's circle of acquaintances.

Fourth, when I saw that I had made a mistake, I took action to correct it. Asking someone to leave your employment can be a very difficult decision, but a business owner must take action to keep the business from deteriorating further.

Fifth, I learned to include in all our letters of employment a statement that the employee is hired "at will." My companies also instituted a formal evaluation process to be completed in the first ninety days after hire for all employees, even for high level executives. If new hires receive favorable evaluations after their first ninety days, they still continue employment "at will." In the case of the CFO, I had not done a formal evaluation. Clearly this was a failure on my part.

Finally, my experience with these executive hires enlightened me about my own abilities. I am a good strategist, capable of putting together good companies, but I am less effective at handling day-to-day operations and staying focused.

My experience in buying and running businesses overseas taught me that even though the United States is a large marketplace, we should not ignore opportunities available overseas. Admittedly, the language and customs are sometimes quite different, but one should not let these differences get in the way of expanding business opportunities. I also learned that, in many cases, American entrepreneurs are welcomed in overseas business environments because they bring a different mindset to business operations and management.

Hence, I did not pass up a good business opportunity simply because it was in Switzerland. Distance proved to be no real problem either, given today's ease of travel. I found that I could travel from the East Coast to Europe as easily as I could to California. Getting involved initially with Swiss companies convinced me of the importance of having a global vision. The rewards can be significant.

Bringing My Sons into the Business

When my oldest son David was a senior in high school, he asked if he could work at Fidelity during the summer. I offered him three choices: he could work in the custodial department, or in maintenance fixing pipes and other fixtures, or he could be an assistant on the assembly floor. He chose the last option. Later when Chuck and Michael were old enough to work, I offered them the same types of summer jobs. They also took me up on my offer. Of course, this kind of work was not always fun. David remembers working in shipping and receiving and operating the fork lift. Michael spent part of one summer working in the copy room. For eight hours each day he copied contracts, creating printed documents from microfilms. What the boys may not have realized is that they were learning how the business works "from the ground up." I always had hoped that they would enter the business someday, and I wanted them to be prepared with a sound work ethic and an understanding of business at Fidelity Technologies.

After graduating from Phoenixville Area High School, David went to college at Lyndon State College, in Vermont. He seemed to enjoy the New England environment, but he found he was too far away from his girlfriend, Loretta (Lori) Way, who attended Slippery Rock University in western Pennsylvania. He wanted to move closer to her, but I think he was afraid that I would be disappointed in him if he left Lyndon State. It was with some trepidation that he asked me if he could transfer. I was not at all unhappy that he wished to change schools; I simply wanted him to earn a college degree. He transferred to West Chester University in southeastern Pennsylvania, which was close to home and not as far away from Lori. However, the transfer did add extra time to his schooling. He graduated in 1993.

Although being in college made him less available to work at Fidelity, he returned occasionally during breaks. He was an average student at West Chester University, and his Physical Education major did not prepare him for employment in business. Nevertheless, while he was in college, he and a friend started their own successful business during the summer: Dave & John's Handyman Service. Their company slogan was, "We will do what you don't want to do." That told me he was not averse to working, and he had some business savvy.

At some point I decided that, if any of my sons wanted to work in any type of management position at Fidelity Technologies, they would have to work elsewhere for three years. Naturally I hoped that all three sons would pursue useful and financially rewarding careers, and then perhaps join me at Fidelity Technologies if they were still interested in doing so. I knew it would be unwise to bring them into the company immediately upon completing their studies. To be effective working for me, they would first have to learn what it meant to be in the work force under someone else's tutelage.

David's path to a position at Fidelity began on the day he graduated from West Chester University. Although he had aspired to become a physical education teacher, his student teaching experiences had convinced him that he was not cut out for that kind of work, with its constant repetition of lessons and its regimented routines. Knowing he had not yet secured a job, after his graduation ceremony I offered him work at Cossonay, the Swiss company I had purchased a year earlier. He accepted immediately. Within a few weeks we had made arrangements for David to move to Switzerland. Rosemary and I traveled to Europe with all three boys. We enjoyed a two-week vacation touring Venice, Florence, and Rome, and skiing at Zermatt in the Swiss Alps. Then we headed to Lausanne to help David move into the apartment I had already rented. It was not furnished, but we helped him secure some basics.

David's first experience with the Swiss way of doing business taught him an important lesson. He had problems being certified for his new job in marketing and sales. The day he walked in he did not have the official credentials showing that he had completed his degree. He had not paid a library fine nor provided to West Chester University documentation of his internship at a summer camp. Following the trip, Rosemary had to track down the paperwork from his internship and pay the library fine, so that the University would provide the official documentation of his degree.

In the fall, Lori visited David in Switzerland. They became engaged and set a date for their wedding. After they married the next July, Lori accompanied David back to Lausanne, where they stayed for nearly three years. Their oldest son, our first grandchild, Jack David Gulati III, was born in Switzerland.

Jack reading to grandson David, age 2.

After working for two years in sales and marketing, David eventually took over as interim general manager of Cossonay. In 1995 I told him I was planning to close down Cossonay's operations in Switzerland and bring the company to Reading, to merge it into Fidelity Technologies. I asked if he would like to be in charge of arranging this move. The task involved assembling a team to move the assets, including inventory, machinery, equipment, customer files, and records, while still keeping the business going to satisfy customers' needs. It was a tough, time-sensitive challenge because it involved an international transfer of sophisticated, heavy machinery and equipment. All components had to be broken down, transported by ship, and reassembled in Reading in a timely manner. He accomplished this task splendidly; not a single product shipment date was compromised.

Shortly after David's return to Pennsylvania, I converted the U.S. branch of Cossonay Meteorology into the Meteorology Division of Fidelity Technologies, and put David in charge. He stayed with the Meteorology Division for three years, until I asked him to manage Fidelity TeleAlarm, the U.S. distribution center for the products we manufactured at Telectronic in Switzerland. The success of David's efforts to manage Fidelity's Meteorology Division is evidenced by its remaining a key part of Fidelity Technologies today.

Two years after David finished his undergraduate education, Chuck completed his degree at West Chester University as well. He had started at Kutztown University in Berks County, Pennsylvania, but transferred after a year to West Chester's Criminal Justice program. He was a middle-of-the-road student during his first two years in college and was unable to focus, so he took a break and came to live with Rosemary and me. We charged him no rent but insisted he get a job. He found work with The Vanguard Group in Malvern, Pennsylvania. After a year, with a new sense of personal responsibility, he returned to West Chester University where he made the dean's list in his final two years. As part of the curriculum, he completed an internship with the Pennsylvania Parole Board in Chester, Pennsylvania. He intended to make a career in the criminal justice system, but after being on patrol with a sheriff to round up a convict, gunshots were exchanged, and Chuck thought better of this career choice.

After graduation in 1995 Chuck accepted a position at Telectronic in Switzerland. To prepare for this job, he first spent a few months at Fidelity TeleAlarm in the United States. He then moved to Switzerland where he interned in the technical department at Telectronic. However, after three months in Europe he became homesick and returned home. He took a succession of short-term jobs, first in north New Jersey with Chrysler Financial Corporation as a collections specialist; there he was a stellar employee. Next he followed his long-time desire to work with troubled youth. He became a residential counselor with the Devereux Foundation, a national behavioral health organization founded to help youth and their families.

Finally, in 1998 Chuck returned to work at Fidelity TeleAlarm where he handled a variety of assignments over a four-year span. These were lower-level management positions, but he did well. He then accepted the assignment to establish Avalon Technologies in Charlottesville, Virginia, a new company created from the assets I had acquired earlier, and he served as General Manager. During this period he met a lovely girl, Jennifer Candalore, and they married in 2000. In 2002, he moved to Fidelity Technologies to join his brothers in the company that I was planning eventually to turn over to them.

Our third son, Michael, graduated from Malvern Preparatory School. He was much better prepared for college than either of his brothers. Michael enrolled at Babson, a very fine business college in Wellesley, Massachusetts. He did well there, graduating in four years. Although his mother encouraged him to major in finance because he had a good head for numbers, he chose to study marketing and entrepreneurship. Perhaps he was preparing himself for his future with Fidelity Technologies; unlike his older brothers, he had decided while still in high school that he would like to work there or go out on his own if a position at Fidelity did not materialize. When he graduated in 1997, he received a number of job offers and asked me for advice on which to accept. There were offers from a major accounting firm, from K-Mart, and from a major bank. I recommended he take a position at K-Mart in their management training program.

Michael's choice of employment may sound strange, but I had good reason to make this recommendation. I followed the advice of advisory board member, General Jack Vessey. I had mentioned Michael's dilemma to General Vessey, and he immediately recommended that Michael accept the offer from K-Mart. I asked, "Why?" He pointed out that stores such as K-Mart are where "real America" meets and shops; by working there Michael will come to understand the lifestyles and problems of middle-America. On reflection I thought this made sense, and so did Michael.

Michael was well liked at K-Mart, and in two years moved into management. He was placed in charge of a good-sized store, and he did well. At this point he asked if he, too, could come into the business. Although he was a few months shy of being employed three years elsewhere, I bent my rule and allowed him to join Fidelity Technologies. In 2000, he began at Fidelity as a cost accountant.

Michael *(center)* **with his brothers and best men at his wedding in 2005, David** *(left)* **and Charles** *(right). (Photo by Pat's Studio)*

Within months of Michael's arrival at Fidelity, the vice president for finance quit. Michael then began reporting to our Controller, and he assumed responsibility for preparing detailed financial reports. His employees loved him. He demonstrated great analytical skills and devoted time to learning the business. Michael had an easy-going management style; he sought help from his colleagues so he could learn to be their supervisor. He built great loyalty in his division, and most of the people who worked there in 1997 when he started are still with the company. While he worked principally for Fidelity Technologies, Michael also prepared monthly financial reports for my European companies, serving in effect as Fidelity Group's financial manager. When the Controller left to start her own business, Mike took over as Controller, a position he held until 2004, when he became Vice President of Finance.

Developing a Succession Plan

By 2001 I had placed Fidelity Technologies on sound footing, made some other acquisitions, and solidified operations in the TeleAlarm Group. At approximately the same time we also made several important changes in our Advisory Board. In 2000, Stan Kabala, a former president of Rogers Cantel Communications, Canada's largest wireless company, joined the Board. Stan had most recently been chairman and CEO of Executone, the voice and data systems company in Connecticut. He had retired, and was now living in Naples, Florida. In 2001, Bill Chorske resigned, and we added two new members: Dan Luthringhauser and Karl Bornschein. Luthringhauser was the former vice president and general manager of Medtronic, Inc. and had extensive experience with Medtronic's European division. When he joined our board, he was serving as principal and senior executive of DRL International, an international consulting firm. Bornschein was Medtronic's Vice President for Central Europe. He worked at Medtronic's European headquarters, first located in Belgium and later relocated to Lausanne, Switzerland. Bornschein was an Honorary Senator in the European Academy of Sciences and Arts, a trans-national organization promoting interdisciplinary discussion and visionary thinking on issues affecting the future of Europe.

As I approached my sixtieth birthday, it was time to turn my attention to another important matter that the board had been prompting me to consider for some time: "What have you done about succession planning?" The most insistent voice prodding me to think about succession came from Stan Kabala. He was one of the most vocal board members asking me to give serious consideration to my succession.

Initially, I had designated Al Jodzio as the one who would take over in my absence; I also identified others who would be in line after him. My sons were not in the picture yet. Of course, I had always assumed I would pass on my business to them, if they so desired and were competent. That is, after all, a centuries-old Indian custom, and from the time my oldest was born, I had, in the back of my mind the notion that one reason to build a successful business was to establish a legacy for succeeding generations of my family in the United States, my adopted home. Now that I had been encouraged to think actively about succession planning, I considered my options. Passing on the business to my sons was high on the list, although I did not see that as viable at the moment. Naturally, I could sell the business outright if I wanted to get a lump-sum settlement and simply go into retirement. In addition, I could try to take the company public. As a publicly traded company, Fidelity would have a new Board of Directors who would be responsible for identifying my successor as head of the company when I stepped down. Likewise, I could seek a merger, preferably with a competitor who would understand our business and continue operations with little disruption. The pros and cons of each of these options, and some others besides, are discussed at length in the next part of this book.

Before making any decision, I discussed the matter at some length with Rosemary. It was apparent that the business had considerable value. Since Rosemary and I were sole owners, the business was, in essence, a notable inheritance, something worth protecting. Rosemary encouraged me to make plans so that, in the event that something happened to me, our sons would not end up squabbling over the business. We decided that, whatever happened, the boys would own the business equally—whether they worked together in it or not. When I told the board of our family decision, they asked: "So what are your plans for the boys?"

The board saw potential in Mike, who had appeared at board meetings to make financial presentations. On more than one occasion, they told me that one day Mike would be a dynamite CFO for a large company. He could communicate well, held his own in arguments without being confrontational, and knew the company's finances inside out. Most importantly, he was a good listener and consistently adhered to the board's sound advice. I then decided to invite my oldest son, David, to board meetings to make presentations on Fidelity TeleAlarm and participate in the entire meeting. After they had met with him several times, board members said David seemed to have excellent leadership potential but, despite his excellent work running Fidelity TeleAlarm, he lacked the educational skills and background to hold a top-level position in a large, complex company like Fidelity Technologies. At this point Chuck was not fully invested in the company, but I had to make appropriate plans to account for the possibility that he, too, might want to take on an executive role at some date.

The board and I spoke with David and told him that if he wanted to become a senior executive, he would have to earn an MBA. The board recommended that he accomplish his advanced education in the shortest possible time. Therefore, it was decided that he go back to school full-time. The company would pay his tuition and fees. David chose to enroll in the Haub School of Business at St. Joseph's University in Philadelphia. This choice allowed him to live at home with his family, and gave him the necessary time to concentrate on studies. While he was getting his degree, he spent time during the summer completing projects for Fidelity and reporting to the board. These presentations impressed the board greatly. They noticed the change in David over the two years he had been in school. When he graduated with an MBA, he came back to the company. The board did not think he was ready to become CEO; therefore, he was assigned to the COO position where he worked directly under Stan Kabala, who filled in for me as temporary CEO while I took a sabbatical during 2003.

The idea that I should take a sabbatical came about as a result of my telling the board that I was contemplating retirement at age sixty-four or sixty-five. Several board members chided me for thinking I could retire at all. A number of them had continued working past age seventy, and they thought I, too, would want to remain in business well beyond my sixty-fifth birthday. To help me make a decision, they encouraged me to take a sabbatical. Stan Kabala, who knew the business quite well and had served as CEO of a similar business, offered to run the company for six months while I was away. I asked Stan to step out of the meeting, so that the rest of the board could discuss his offer openly. After a short discussion Jack Vessey stated that Stan had made a most gracious offer, and the rest of the board enthusiastically endorsed the idea. Stan found an apartment and moved temporarily to Reading, and I embarked on a quest to see how I might move into retirement.

The sabbatical was a godsend personally, but it also served another purpose, one that proved vitally important to Fidelity Technologies. During the time I was gone, Kabala had a chance to observe David's and Michael's work habits, and evaluate their fitness to take over operations at the company. After supervising them for six months, he reported to the board that he thought they were ready to step in and run the show.

On January 1, 2004, I sold the company to the three boys. They paid me the full, fair market value that I would have received from any other outside party. However, I allowed them

Dave Gulati presents an oil portrait of Jack sitting at his desk at Fidelity Technologies. Portrait was commissioned by his three sons to commemorate the sale of the company to them. Portrait hangs in the entrance to the Fidelity building. *(Artist: Jim Riley, 2004)*

to pay in quarterly payments, while still keeping a security interest in the shares of the company until it was paid in full. Each of my three sons owned equal shares. The next big decision was: What role would each fill? I did not want to create rivalries, so we talked at length about the best way to assign leadership roles. I suggested that they might want to rotate the presidency among themselves every two years. That method had worked in other companies with which I was familiar. Setting up a two-year cycle would allow each to put his mark on the company but not keep any one brother in the top seat for too long. Being away from the top job for four years would give each son time to reflect on accomplishments and decide how to improve the company's performance.

The brothers considered my suggestion but decided instead that David should serve as president. He had the personal and leadership skills to handle the job. Mike's skills lay in finance, so he would become the company's chief financial officer. Chuck was not too sure yet what his ultimate position would be, but on an interim basis he assumed the position of Operations Manager. There was a possibility that he would leave the company but maintain ownership. I recommended that if Chuck were to follow that plan, he should receive ownership at the current market value, but that his brothers would share the increased market value, since they would be the principal contributors to the company's growth. Chuck seemed unsure of what to do. His brothers told him that, while he was working effectively as an operational manager, he would need more education if he wanted to be an effective executive. They suggested that, like David, he earn an MBA. Chuck was amenable to the idea. He could see the difference an MBA had made to David in the way he conducted business and in his analytical skills. His brothers told Chuck he had to go to a top-notch school full-time. Mike and David agreed that the company would pay for Chuck's education, just as it had for David. Not surprisingly, however, when he investigated the requirements for enrolling at a nationally renowned institution, he discovered he was lacking some of the prerequisites.

To his credit, Chuck did not let that stop him. Instead, he enrolled at Montgomery County Community College on his own time, at night, while continuing to work full-time. Completing the prerequisite coursework would qualify him for admission to universities such as the Wharton School at the University of Pennsylvania, the Darden School at the University of Virginia, the Tuck School of Business at Dartmouth, or the Smeal College of Business at Penn State. Additionally, he enrolled in Kaplan's program to prepare for the GMAT to insure that he would score high enough on this examination to convince these institutions to take a chance on him. After two years of prep work, he applied and was admitted to his first choice—Penn State. It was a superb choice because his wife was an alumna and knew the place well, and it was close enough to home and work that he could keep in touch easily. He locked up his house and moved his family, including two small children, to University Park, where he rented an apartment and began a rigorous two-year program of study.

Chuck was an honor student at Penn State. As part of the curriculum, students were required to obtain summer internship positions with major corporations. Chuck landed an internship at DuPont in Delaware. He did a superb job for DuPont, and upon graduation he was offered a position involving domestic and international assignments, with a good salary and career path. Frankly, the offer floored me, it was so generous. In addition,

Chuck's reputation at Penn State earned him an invitation a year after graduation to join the MBA Alumni Advisory Board at the Smeal School of Business.

Chuck's brothers met with him to see whether he was serious about going with DuPont or coming back to Fidelity as part of the management team. I thought Chuck should take the DuPont offer; the salary and benefits were substantially more than Fidelity could propose. On the other hand, David and Michael put together a package for Chuck that was in some ways comparable to what DuPont was offering. They really wanted him back helping them grow the business. Chuck was asked to manage the Military & Aerospace Manufacturing Division. The division was losing money and had produced few innovations. There was a chance that the company would sell off or close this division; feelers were sent out to see if there were interested buyers. There were no takers, so Chuck developed a strategy for improving the division's operations, aligning the division's capabilities with the product lines the Military & Aerospace Manufacturing Division should pursue. Within six months he had won a government contract for the PDISE unit with a potential value of $120 million in revenues, a huge coup for this small division. PDISE stands for Power Distribution Illumination System Electrical and is used to subdivide and distribute electricity from single power sources to multiple equipment users within shelters and various unit complexes. This success presented another kind of conundrum. The division was now worth considerably more than it had been when David and Michael initially tried to sell it. Mike did an analysis of the profit margins on this contract so the brothers could make a considered judgment about the division's value to Fidelity Technologies. Should they offer it for sale with its new, lucrative contract, perhaps attracting a handsome profit now? Or should they keep it and see if, under Chuck's leadership, the Military & Aerospace Division would be an even more valuable asset over the long term?

The boys decided to consult their Board of Advisors, which now had only three members. Shortly after my sons took over the company, they decided to dissolve the advisory board since they no longer needed expertise in all the fields covered by the five-member board I had assembled. Later they reconstituted a board consisting of Stan Kabala, Dan Luthringhauser, and myself. This group helped them evaluate their options.

My sons knew that any potential buyer would conduct extensive due diligence and demand some guarantees that the projected business would generate the kinds of revenues expected from the new contract. Fidelity had three options:

1. Continue operations in the division with the same level of resources and try to generate maximum profit margins but forego opportunities to add additional business within the division;
2. Simply run out the contract in the normal environment;
3. Give Chuck additional resources to see how he could parlay this contract into additional business and generate a long-term product line for the company.

Dave and Mike's first recommendation was to sell the division to outsiders, followed by fulfilling the contract but adding no new business. The advisory board, on the other hand, had a different recommendation. They suggested that Chuck be allowed to develop a business plan showing how, if he were given additional money, he could build the division over time. The brothers listened to their advisors and decided to let Chuck have his head, so to speak, in growing the division. Since that date, the original contract has generated approximately $100 million in gross revenues and significant profits for the company. The lesson here is that, if there's an opportunity, a business needs to make the necessary investments to take advantage.

Armed with this vote of confidence, Chuck became a very good manager. By 2010 his division produced the company's highest gross revenues and was the company's most profitable division. In 2012, this division was commemorated for having shipped 10,000 PDISE units. Additionally, the decision to invest in the division kept the company in the manufacturing

Celebrating the delivery of the 10,000th PDISE unit: left to right: Robert Thoens, Product Director, U.S. Army; Robert Lesko, General Manager, Military and Aerospace Division, Fidelity Technologies; Col. Brian Cummings, Project Manager, U.S. Army; William Sverapa, Deputy Program Executive Officer, U.S. Army; Carol Obando-Derstine, Regional Manager, office of U. S. Senator Robert P. Casey, Jr.; David Gulati, President, Fidelity Technologies; Congressman James Gerlach, 6th District, Pennsylvania.

line of work. The company now had three divisions: Military & Aerospace Manufacturing, Simulation & Training, and Field Services, but they were all interconnected and operated as a homogeneous unit. I had originally told my sons that it would be rare that all three divisions would operate "in high gear" simultaneously every year. There would always be times when one division would underperform. Therefore, it was important to keep all three going, so that when one slumped, the others could carry the company.

The company I sold to my sons on January 1, 2004 had revenues of $23+ million and had approximately 200 employees. In 2011, under my sons' leadership for seven years, Fidelity Technologies had revenues in excess of $110 million, and employed approximately 650 people. In addition to securing a number of important contracts, Fidelity was recognized as a "top 100" company by Military Training Technology for its contributions to military training, and was cited as a leader in the simulation and training industry. Furthermore, they named Fidelity's Call for Fire Trainer (CFFT) a "best program." In 2010, the company received a certificate of appreciation from the U.S. Army for its support of Combined Arms Tactical Trainers (CATT).

In 2010, Fidelity Technologies was named by Deloitte & Touche LLP as one of the top fifty technology companies in the Greater Philadelphia area and was honored by the U.S. Small Business Administration as winner of the SBA's Philadelphia District Office's "Celebrate Success" initiative for Berks County, Pennsylvania. The following year the company was ranked No. 16 on Deloitte & Touche's list of "Fast Fifty" companies in the Greater Philadelphia area, and No. 394 on the national "Fast 500" list. In 2011 Inc. Magazine placed Fidelity on its "top 5000" list for the third year in a row. This list is considered the "gold standard" of private business success. Each year Fidelity has moved higher on the list. Its 2011 ranking as No. 1412 places it in the top 28 percent of the nation's privately held businesses.

Closer to home, in 2010 Fidelity Technologies was ranked #1 on the Greater Reading Chamber of Commerce Top Business Awards list. In 2011 the company came in at #2 for the same award. I am exceptionally proud of my sons' achievements, but I believe that I put them in a position to succeed by building a solid foundation from which they could grow the company. They, too, have faced some tough times, but they have handled the stresses of business with aplomb and a calm demeanor that reflects confidence in their ability to succeed in the ever-changing environment of the high-tech world of defense contracting.

Quite a few people told me that I was not really retiring, and that I would still be pulling the strings at Fidelity Technologies. But a fundamental principle I learned from my board was to say goodbye graciously and then disappear. On the day I sold the company, I said my farewells to the staff. I shared some of my monetary rewards with them and told them that my sons were now in charge. My board had suggested that I move my office out of the building so people would not think "Jack's still here." Although I did not move out, my new office was physically separated from the major sections of Fidelity's business.

I believe the way in which I left the company was the right move. I told my sons I would not come to them with advice. However, if they wished to seek my counsel, they could call me at any time. I have managed to follow that principle since leaving. I encouraged my sons not to be afraid of making decisions, and told them that if they discover they have made a wrong decision, they should not hesitate to change course. I have seen so many people in companies, especially larger ones, bury their wrong decisions. They end up pouring in more money to justify their original decision, and start the "blame game." Even when this method succeeds, it most frequently does so at someone else's expense. Besides, I have learned from experience that it is impossible to play the "blame game" forever.

I also encouraged my sons to manage the business conservatively, not to overspend or be flashy or demand a corner office and $10,000 in furniture. I cautioned them to maintain a lean staff, even when the business is going well, because bureaucracy will grow exponentially when allowed to flourish.

> **Lessons Learned:** *Determining what will happen to your business once you are no longer involved is perhaps the most critical decision an entrepreneur needs to make. Uncertainty is inherent in life, and none of us can be certain how long we will continue in our businesses. Therefore, you need an exit plan. Looking back, I can say with some degree of satisfaction that succession planning worked at Fidelity Technologies. However, not everyone will pass on a business to children or other relatives. That is why it is critical to start planning early— perhaps as soon as you go into business—when and how you will transfer ownership and operational management of your company when you are either unable to continue or wish to pursue other opportunities.*

Life after Fidelity Technologies Corporation

Although I sold Fidelity Technologies in 2004, I still held on to the TeleAlarm Group that I had formed several years earlier. The companies in this group were based largely in Europe. It took me approximately two more years to get that business into a position where I felt it would survive and thrive without me. I was getting tired of traveling back and forth to Europe, even though when I arrived there, I felt energized and still enjoyed engaging in negotiations. The tougher these were, the more I liked participating. My plan was to retire in 2007 at age 65. Therefore, I negotiated a deal to sell the TeleAlarm Group to Bosch, a German conglomerate, for a handsome price—enough that I no longer had to worry about ever having to work again. I sold TeleAlarm Group at a particularly fortuitous time. Business worldwide was booming, and I was able to take advantage of the current trend toward mergers by selling out when one could still make a substantial profit from companies eager to increase their holdings. As I had learned earlier in my business career, I knew that "timing is everything," and that my time was now. Several of the major companies in the industry had already merged and amassed a great deal of power to control the market. I was a second-tier company in this industry, while at the time Bosch, in my opinion, was in the third tier. I originally made overtures to buy Bosch's TeleCare division because we were both too small to compete effectively in the current marketplace for Personal Emergency Response Systems (PERS). As it turned out, they made a counteroffer to buy me out. After some tough negotiations we settled on a price, which was to remain undisclosed, and closed the deal on September 29, 2006. I walked away from this company as I had from Fidelity.

I signed a "non-compete" clause that precluded me from being in the same business for three years. That did not bother me at all because I planned to fully retire. I intended to spend winters in our home in Bonita Springs, Florida, spring and fall in our home in Oley, Pennsylvania, and summers in Avalon, New Jersey. We had bought our Florida home somewhat sooner than we planned. Once we had settled on southwest Florida as the place for our retirement, we had three criteria: I wanted navigable waterfront so I could engage in boating; we had to be in a community that offered golf membership; and we had to find a location which provided an easy commute by air back to Pennsylvania, where our family lives. Our original plan was to rent for a few years until we found just the right place.

However, things changed fast when I received a postcard in the mail, informing me that a property in the Bonita Bay community in Bonita Springs on the west coast of Florida was to be auctioned in a few weeks. The community offered golfing, and this particular property was on the Imperial River, a navigational waterway only fifteen minutes from the Gulf of Mexico. I called

Stan Kabala, who lived in nearby Naples, and requested that he look at the property. He called back with an enthusiastic report. He said the location was perfect for our needs. The homes in this development were going for $2 million and up. Coincidentally, Rosemary's sister and her husband had just bought a small place in a "55 and over" community in nearby Estero. I did some homework to see what I should offer as a respectable bid at the auction, researched taxes and living conditions in the area, and then traveled to Florida one day before the auction to do some on-site investigation and talk with the agent handling the sale. I learned that the owner of the property was a "flipper." He had purchased a number of properties in Florida but had overextended himself. I knew a decent bid would be accepted because the owner needed to get out from under his debts.

At the auction I was the highest bidder at $1,000,000. However, the owner had the right to refuse the highest bid if he

Bonita Springs home in Florida purchased at auction in 2005.

did not think it matched his undisclosed minimum price. To my delight, the owner accepted the bid. My friends could not believe my good fortune. We had not planned to buy a retirement home this early, but we could not pass up the opportunity. Rosemary spent the next two years getting the house furnished and decorated, while I wrapped up my business affairs and prepared for retirement.

After I sold my European business in 2006, at age 64, I once again experimented with retirement. I was sure this time I would succeed. I started growing a ponytail (which I learned takes two years to grow) and settled in to enjoy my new freedom.

Retirement did not last long. I soon realized that sitting around doing nothing was not for me—at least not yet. So in 2007 I bought the assets of SafetyCare Inc., a company located in Hackensack, New Jersey, with whom TeleAlarm had established a strategic alliance in 2005. I made this purchase through SafetyCare Technologies LLC, a new company I created specifically to acquire the assets and launch a new business venture. The idea behind the new company was to provide monitoring services for seniors living independently. There seemed great potential for this kind of business. The world's population was getting older, and many people wanted to continue living independently. At the same time, government simply did not have the resources to take care of the aging population. Placing monitoring devices in individual homes would be attractive to seniors who would know someone "on the other end" would be available should they need help in an emergency, or want to have vital signs checked routinely. The business model was to provide monitoring services directly to the clients, as opposed to selling products. The distinguishing feature that would separate SafetyCare from other providers in the industry was that we would staff our call center with certified Emergency Medical Technicians (EMTs) rather than using the typical call center screeners.

Buying assets and setting up a company on paper is a far cry from getting the business up and running. Our first challenge with SafetyCare was to create a space for our emergency call center. We decided to renovate the last remaining space in the Fidelity Technologies building—space that had been sealed off because it had housed the ovens for the old Bachman Pretzel factory. This area contained asbestos and lead paint that had to be removed in accordance with federal and state regulations to assure that those who would be working in the building would not be exposed to harmful substances. After the space had been cleared of harmful substances, the entire area was renovated and equipped as a state-of-the-art call center. SafetyCare Technologies began operating in the renovated facility on September 20, 2007.

What I have learned from SafetyCare, and from some of my other businesses as well, is that when getting into an industry that is just being created, it is best to try to get ahead of the curve, but not too far ahead. Often, the first generation of companies in an industry struggles to be innovative, while the next generation comes to market and reaps the benefits from those initial innovations. Hence, it is always best to be just behind the leading edge. For example, in the computer industry, Univac was a pioneer, but IBM made the money. In personal computers, several companies entered the market early with some initial innovations, but Microsoft and Apple capitalized on what those early developers learned and captured the market. Similar examples can be found in the airline industry where the early airlines became dinosaurs as new companies developed better business models to take advantage of new technologies and the changing market place. Lastly, in the photocopy business, 3M created the technology for photocopying, but Xerox captured the market.

What happens consistently is that the first generation of businesses puts so much of its resources into developing the demand for its product that it often finds itself behind the curve in innovation. The second generation in an industry does not have to worry about creating market demand but can focus on "building a better mousetrap" to serve customers' requirements.

Lesson Learned: *Regardless of the industry, creating a market demand for a new product is very expensive. But after the first-generation companies have done this kind of heavy lifting, it is possible to enter an industry and do quite well with a product that is technologically ahead of its competition and meets customers' needs. To do so, however, requires the entrepreneur to be continually looking for opportunities in emerging industries or in areas where new technologies are revolutionizing business practices. Knowing when to enter a certain market is as much an art as it is a science, but if one keeps abreast of business developments, it is possible to make intelligent decisions about the right time to launch a new venture in an area that shows promise.*

When I started SafetyCare, I began slowly, trying to tap into the marketplace for services and devices that allow seniors to live independently. I had well-developed reasons for this strategy, knowing that the world population would continue to age, and the

SafetyCare General Manager, Drew Bell *(center)*, **and Paul Newiadomy, EMT Operator** *(seated)*, **in discussions with Jack** *(right)* **at the SafetyCare Monitoring Center .**

peak for sales in this market would be reached around 2020. I wanted to position my company so that our technology would be accepted and demanded by customers as the market matured. The next generation of services and products was expected to be "TeleCare," whereby sensors installed in homes would monitor whether people were active, and whether heating and cooling systems, appliances, and the like were operating properly. Information from these sensors would be transmitted to a monitoring center that would provide two-way communication with the elderly person living independently. The next step in the evolution of this business model will be "Telemedicine," the use of telecommunication and information technologies to monitor blood pressure, weight, and other vital signs remotely. This information will be transmitted immediately to a health care facility where trained medical advisors will review the information and take appropriate actions.

To take advantage of these trends, in the beginning of 2010 I bought two Swiss companies, Transrex AG, located in Zug, and Synapse, located in Biel. Tibor Ganyi, my former colleague from TeleAlarm, was now the General Manager at Transrex. He alerted me that Transrex may be available to purchase. Claude Romy, who had gone on to form his own company specializing in merger and acquisitions, brought Synapse to my attention. With collaboration from Ganyi I was successful in purchasing these two companies. Transrex manufactured equipment used in hospitals and clinics for communication and entertainment, incorporating television, internet, and phone service into one bedside console. Synapse, on the other hand, manufactured a watch-based transmitter used in personal emergency response systems. At the end of 2010, I merged Synapse into Transrex and appointed Tibor Ganyi as the General Manager of the new Transrex. These companies employed trusted, first-rate research and development engineers who could develop cutting-edge products. Therefore, I could continue to develop an integrated system of personal healthcare devices that would be ready for market when demand for such items increased.

Personal Emergency Response System manufactured by Transrex SA in Switzerland.

World's first accurate Fall Detector manufactured by Transrex SA in Switzerland.

Lesson Learned: *An entrepreneur should go where the expertise is and not be geographically bound. After all, Europe is not significantly farther from Philadelphia, New York, or Miami than California. In addition, starting SafetyCare has convinced me that, to be successful, a business must control both the product and the service. Only in an ideal partnership can these elements be split. It is not necessary to own both segments, but control is essential. Only by having a say in the total process can the entrepreneur influence the entire supply chain. Every piece need not be in place on day one, but the strategy must incorporate this goal, as well as provide the resources to achieve it.*

Purchasing Stokesay Castle:
Never Too Old to Learn New Things

In 2009, I learned that Stokesay Castle, a historic, English-style castle converted into a restaurant in Reading, Pennsylvania, was going up for auction. This news immediately brought back memories. I had been fascinated with the possibilities of this place for nearly two decades, and had even expressed interest in purchasing it some years earlier. Now, I contemplated, at this stage in my life, if I wanted to start a new venture in a field where I had no previous experience.

Stokesay Castle had been an icon in Reading for eighty years. In 1931, Reading businessman George Hiester, heir to the Reading Railroad fortune, built a replica of the original Stokesay Castle, a 13th century structure in southern England, on a mountain overlooking the city of Reading. Hiester intended the place to be a surprise wedding present for his new bride. Unfortunately, she did not like the completed structure, and the couple spent little time there. In 1956 the castle was sold and converted into a high-end restaurant; a banquet hall was later

Stokesay Castle, Reading, Pennsylvania. *(Photo by Secoges Photographics)*

added, and the owners began hosting corporate events and private functions. For three decades Stokesay Castle was regarded by the people of Reading and surrounding Berks County as "the place to go" for fine dining and special occasions.

Unfortunately, in the 1990s Stokesay Castle began going downhill. In 1991 I experienced first-hand the sad state into which the castle had declined. By that time Fidelity Technologies employed about ten individuals, and we decided to schedule our Christmas party at Stokesay. When we arrived, we discovered that the room we had reserved had not been set up; it took the restaurant staff quite some time to ready the room. The food was passable, but we learned later that the roast beef we had ordered for dinner had been dropped on the floor, picked up, and served. I did not go back to Stokesay Castle for a decade. However, in 2003 I had some important guests in town, and I decided that, despite my bad experience earlier, I would take them there because it was a landmark destination in Berks County. We had lunch in the main dining room. Sadly, only one other table was occupied, and the room appeared dingy and dirty. It was obvious that the place had gone further downhill.

Six months later, I inquired if Stokesay Castle might be for sale. The question that immediately comes to mind is, "Why"? What would make me want to purchase a place that was deteriorating rapidly and which had not met even modest expectations for quality or service? The answer provides a lesson for entrepreneurs who can look past cosmetic problems to see the core potential of a business. I could see that the place had possibilities, but it was not being run efficiently. It was certainly not generating the revenues that could be realized if the operation were well run. I also knew that, despite the facility's recent troubles, many local residents had fond memories of earlier times at Stokesay Castle. Many couples were married there and had their wedding receptions in the grand hall or on the grounds. Companies held annual events at Stokesay. Countless business people and families could recall eating a great meal there, or strolling around the grounds to get a glimpse of the city and the surrounding countryside below. The place simply needed a strong management team with a vision for restoring the "Stokesay brand."

This first overture was rejected. A year later, however, I came to know an attorney who represented the owners, so I asked again if the owners would be willing to sell. This time the answer was yes, but the asking price was $5.5 million. I am not sure that I had any number in mind, but this asking price was certainly far too high, considering all the work that would need to be done to make the place presentable. When the parties are so far apart, negotiations most likely will not be fruitful; therefore, I did not pursue the issue. I decided to bide my time and hope that a more favorable opportunity would materialize.

In 2007, Stokesay Castle closed, and the owners listed the castle with a real estate broker. The asking price was now $3.2 million, a more reasonable price, and I sought information so we could begin a conversation about a purchase. No information ever arrived. I called twice more, and, not receiving the requested information, once again let the idea go.

Eventually, in February 2009, while I was in Florida, I received an email from an auction company that a bankruptcy court had ordered Stokesay Castle to be sold at auction. I was surprised. I was not sure at this point that I wanted to get involved in a new venture. By coincidence, I had to be in Reading the day before the auction, so I decided to conduct some preliminary investigation to determine the maximum amount I might offer. Stokesay was being sold at an "absolute auction," subject to Bankruptcy Court approval. Since the Bankruptcy Court was involved, there was very little chance that the Court would reject the winning bid. The trustee for the auction provided all the information I requested rapidly. I reviewed the documentation, and I liked what I saw. I arranged to have my son David and my contractor, Nick Miller of ProSource Construction, make a property inspection. They reported that Stokesay was in terrible shape but could be cosmetically fixed up for approximately $500,000. The deal now looked feasible, so I decided to travel to Reading a few days earlier, with the intention to participate in the bidding. I was one of four bidders; however, unlike the other three, I was not a seasoned professional in the restaurant business. To my surprise, I was able to purchase the property for $550,000. I also acquired a liquor license for $35,000. By the time I paid taxes and commissions, my total cost was $623,850.

Now that I was committed to buying Stokesay Castle, I started to consider in earnest the renovation requirements and costs. It became clear that I had two options: cosmetic repairs at a cost of $550,000 or a major renovation to make Stokesay a high-end and fully functional restaurant, at a cost of $3,000,000. I reasoned that customers would give us only one chance; if they liked the new Stokesay, they would support us, and if they did not, my restaurant experiment would be a failure. My confidence in this venture received a boost almost as soon as word got out that I had purchased the castle and intended to restore it to its former glory. I was besieged with calls from people who wanted to book events in anticipation of the opening. My assessment of the popularity of the Stokesay brand was proving to be correct, and I thought I had a potential winner on my hands. I decided to do the complete renovation before opening.

The building was stripped down to the bare stone walls, so to speak, and new interior walls, along with new plumbing, electrical wiring, and HVAC systems were installed. In addition, the kitchen was redesigned with new equipment, along with all new dining room furnishings, and a host of other improvements to restore the castle to its original glory. For many years I had maintained a good working relationship on previous construction projects with contractor Nick Miller. I trusted him, and hired him as general contractor to accomplish the myriad renovation projects as quickly as possible.

Learning the Restaurant Business

I knew nothing about the restaurant business and had a lot to learn fast; "rookie" mistakes would be very costly. I knew that in order for Stokesay Castle to operate successfully, I needed to offer great food, exceptional service, and reasonable prices. Therefore, I had to surround myself with highly competent individuals in the business. I first addressed finding an experienced chef with impeccable credentials and reputation. For years I had patronized the Oley Valley Inn, a well-known, high-end, local restaurant in Berks County that had recently closed due to a fire. In years past I had become acquainted with its owner/chef, Steve Yeanish. Almost immediately after the purchase of Stokesay Castle, I approached him, and he agreed to come on board as a consultant. He was instrumental in making initial decisions about the kitchen renovations and recommending suppliers. For the next five months, I visited restaurants, talked with dozens of restaurant owners, chefs and cooks, managers, vendors and especially food suppliers. I shared with them the purpose of our discussions, and to my surprise, all the people I approached were happy to share their expertise with me. I took copious notes.

Armed with new knowledge from my numerous interviews, I started to make some serious staffing decisions. During my "learning period" I had met Willie Brockington, Executive Chef at Reading Country Club. Previously he had received the "Best in Berks" award for banquet facilities from Berks County Living magazine and was also cited by the Philadelphia Food & Wine Society for having flawlessly executed multi-course wine pairing dinners. I was impressed with his credentials, and after some discussion, he agreed to join us as Executive Chef. His first task was to design and equip the kitchen, which he did splendidly.

The greater challenge was to find an excellent General Manager. There was no room for error in this selection; it had to be correct the first time. I needed someone from a top-notch organization, an establishment that was service oriented. After searching for some time, I asked the food and beverage manager at my country club in Bonita Springs, Florida for advice. He recommended two people, and I selected Luis Pereira, who at this time was working and living in Fort Myers, Florida. He was Food & Beverage Director at Verandah Country Club. Previously, he had managed four-star and four-diamond fine dining restaurants, establishments recognized by AAA, Zagat, and Gourmet magazine for excellence in the promotion of wines, food service, supervision of service staff and 100 percent guest satisfaction. He had spent all of his professional life in the hospitality business, having started as a waiter and progressively advancing in his profession. He arrived at Stokesay as General Manager on Labor Day weekend and immediately went to work preparing for the November opening. To complement my previous hires, Luis later hired Andrea Heinly as sous chef. She

Luis Pereira, General Manager, seated on the patio at Stokesay Castle.
(photo by Reading Eagle)

had been a television celebrity on the "Hell's Kitchen" cooking show, where she was third runner-up in 2009. In addition, over the next sixty days, Luis hired approximately 100 employees at all levels of the restaurant.

Before we officially opened on November 7, 2009, we had a number of practice runs. First, we had a special event to celebrate my son David's fortieth birthday. Then, we invited the employees from Fidelity Technologies to a party and sit-down dinner. Lastly, we scheduled a VIP reception for Berks County dignitaries; nearly 400 people attended. We repeated that activity when we opened the outdoor tent bar the following summer. Although one cannot offer too many free promotions without affecting the bottom line, these events paid off for us. Our purpose was to let the community know that this was not the "same old Stokesay Castle"—this was a new place, under new management, with a new operating philosophy. Luis Pereira, Willie Brockington, and I were featured in many articles in local publications and on local radio and television programs. I felt that our team had successfully rehabilitated the "Stokesay brand," and we would be profitable in a short time. For the first few weeks, Stokesay was completely sold out; today for Friday and Saturday dining, one must make reservations weeks in advance.

Lessons Learned: *Purchasing Stokesay has taught me several new lessons and confirmed other beliefs. First, many people thought I was crazy to purchase Stokesay during bad economic times. In my opinion, however, the condition of the economy should not influence those who are prepared to take advantage of business opportunities. When the opportunity presents itself, the savvy entrepreneur will react. I have discovered that, regardless of the economic stresses placed on them, banks are in the business of lending money; it is the job of entrepreneurs to convince bankers that they are trustworthy, and the project is worthy of credit. Entrepreneurs need to take advantage of market conditions and not be scared off by temporary downturns in the economy.*

In the case of Stokesay, my strategy was to demonstrate to the lenders the value of the Stokesay brand and the solid credentials of the management team. I emphasized that if I were to build a new restaurant on the same location, it would have taken several decades to realize the kind of name recognition that Stokesay Castle received immediately. Based on our credentials and the business plan I presented, we received multiple financing offers, even in those tough economic times. Another lesson learned was the importance of good press; we sought and received placement of several positive stories in local and regional publications, much of it before we opened. This publicity proved to be not only good for business, but now the lenders were coming to us.

Finally, I learned that it is possible to go into a business even when one knows little about it, if one has the determination to learn. During the months between purchasing Stokesay Castle and opening for business, I met with dozens of entrepreneurs and restaurant owners to seek their guidance and suggestions. People like to talk about their successes, as long as they know the questioner is seriously interested and not just wasting their time. The combination of expert advice and a dedicated, professional staff that adeptly handles day-to-day operations has made my novice venture successful.

Retirement Again

In 2011, with my seventieth birthday approaching the following year, it was time to pay attention to fulfilling my new goal to retire at age 70. For the past years I had been extremely busy with my six businesses: SafetyCare Technologies LLC, Avalon Technologies LLC, Transrex AG, Stokesay Castle LLC, Stokesay Real Estate LLC, and Fidelity Investment Corporation-Swiss Branch. If I wanted to retire by my seventieth birthday in 2012, it was imperative that I start planning immediately to assure an orderly transfer of ownership; it was already the second half of 2011. As I had done when I decided to sell Fidelity Technologies and TeleAlarm Group, I considered several options and set about to evaluate the best method to divest these companies. I decided to close Fidelity Investment-Swiss Branch because its only asset was the former TeleAlarm building in Le-Chaux-de-Fonds, Switzerland that had just been sold in July 2011. It then immediately became clear that none of the remaining five businesses was large enough or attractive enough to be a candidate for conversion to a public company. Some of those companies were appropriate for sale to third parties, and I had, in fact, received some interest from competitors and venture capitalists.

While I was pondering these possibilities, Rosemary and I had our regularly scheduled meeting with our financial advisor. As part of our estate planning review, we learned that for the tax years of 2011 and 2012, the lifetime federal tax-free gifting exemption per person had been increased from $1 million to $5 million, allowing individuals to give away up to that amount, without the donor or the recipient having to pay any taxes. In our discussions, it became clear that this high exemption would most likely not remain in place past 2012 because of the country's current debt crisis. Based on this information, Rosemary suggested that we consider gifting the five remaining businesses to our three sons. Why not, I thought? We approached our sons, and the three of them discussed the idea among themselves at some length. They thought the companies had potential. Furthermore, they felt that they would have time to manage these additional companies without affecting the operations of Fidelity Technologies. Existing management staff could handle the responsibilities now carried out by one or more of the boys. Specifically, the trio decided that Chuck would transfer from his position as General Manager of the Military & Aerospace Division to become the President of the five companies, and Mike, while keeping his position at Fidelity Technologies, would also act as CFO for the five companies. David, Chuck, and Mike placed only three stipulations on the deal: First, I should make a firm decision shortly, so that they could start developing the 2012 business plan during the fourth quarter of 2011, and begin its implementation at the start of 2012. Second, I had to make a firm commitment not to start or buy any other businesses for the rest of my life. They were well aware of my make-up and figured it likely that I would want to get back in the game before too long. The third condition was that I was not to ask for any free drinks at Stokesay Castle—an inside joke, since we do not allow anyone—even family—free food and beverages there. I cheerfully agreed to the first and third conditions. As to the second condition, I assured them, without making any firm commitments, that at age seventy, the time had come for me to sit back and enjoy the fruits of my labor. The terms seemed to satisfy them, so we closed our preliminary deal on handshakes.

I turned over operating control to them in August 2011, in sufficient time for them to learn the businesses and develop the 2012 business plans. Actual ownership would transfer at the end of the year. The transition time also allowed our accountants and attorneys time to draw up terms of the deal and other necessary paper work. The transition took place as scheduled on December 31, 2011.

Moving into retirement has given me time to think about what I have learned in nearly fifty years as an entrepreneur—about entrepreneurship and about myself. My own experiences have taught me that the key to being a good entrepreneur is to be on the lookout constantly for opportunities to start or buy a new business. Sometimes those opportunities seemed to drop in my lap, but more often I had to create them by doing careful research and looking for ways to innovate. I have discovered that what I have enjoyed most is the chance to get into a new venture, get a business up and running successfully, and then move on. I am less comfortable managing the day-to-day operations of a business that is established and operating smoothly. A good entrepreneur has to recognize his or her strengths and weaknesses and choose his or her professional path wisely.

I believe I have had enough sense to hire good people most of the time and delegate operational responsibilities to them. However, I have always played an active role in strategy and vision for my companies. I have taken great pleasure in negotiating deals and looking for ways to expand my businesses, but I have tried to be realistic and not become too attached to any one of them. There is a time to buy and a time to sell or pass on the business to others; smart entrepreneurs will look for both opportunities.

I have learned that being an entrepreneur sometimes means being unemployed. I was not too proud to survive on unemployment compensation while looking for the next opportunity. Being able to manage one's finances and keep one's family intact when there is no steady income can be a challenge, but it is sometimes necessary. I found that being out of work made me even keener to find the next opportunity to strike out on a new venture.

Looking back, I also see that for every business in which I invested, I researched several dozens more, many of which were far afield from my expertise at the moment. Anyone wishing to be successful as an entrepreneur cannot become too comfortable with one business, or even one industry. The greatest opportunities may lie outside one's current sphere of expertise, but it is possible to learn new skills if one applies oneself diligently and remains optimistic about the chances to succeed.

Knowing how I have lived for the past five decades, I imagine it will be hard for me to stay away from the challenges of business. I am resolved to follow through with my plans for full retirement. Of course, Rosemary tells me she'll believe it when she sees it. Time will tell . . .

PART IV

Some Life Lessons

The foregoing narrative of my career has been intended as an illustration of how a person with vision and determination can be successful in business and family life. In this section I would like to share with readers my thoughts on some topics that are important to every entrepreneur, regardless of the business he or she pursues. You might call it my "accumulated wisdom;" I like to think of these observations as "lessons learned" from a life pursuing my vision to become a successful entrepreneur, who, at the same time built a cohesive family unit. I hope readers will take this advice to heart, and perhaps profit from it.

Balancing Business and Family Life

I never had ulcers or serious heartburn, despite all the tough decisions I had to make. I can remember experiencing fewer than a dozen sleepless nights due to business problems. There was one fundamental principle I learned while in college: I would do anything and everything in the time allotted for my business, but when I arrived home, I would put aside the worries of the business world and concentrate on my family.

My regular work day was usually ten to twelve-hours long, but I can count on two hands the number of days when I took work home with me, and even fewer days when I actually looked at the work I took home. If necessary, I would rather go back to work, even on weekends and holidays, than to feel guilty about bringing work into the home environment. While at home I am a husband and father. When my children were growing up, my routine was to go home, greet my wife and children, and go to my bedroom to change clothes from business attire to "house clothes." That ritual change of clothing worked as a kind of switch, which turned my mind from "work" to "home." I learned this strategy from our first president, George Washington. When he would return home to Mount Vernon, he first took off his uniform and changed to civilian clothes, to signal that he was no longer on duty. Once I was home and had changed clothes, I was able to forget my problems at work and pay attention to my tasks at home. This routine has allowed me to remain stress-free. Over the years I have learned to let tensions go when I move to a different environment. I understand my sons have adopted the same habit.

Communicating with
the Next Generation(s)

How does an entrepreneur bring the second generation into a cohesive family unit? How does he or she share values and thoughts with the third generation? What signs demonstrate that children and grandchildren understand and are adopting the parents' standards? These are the questions I want to answer in this section of the book. Business analyst John Ward makes the point emphatically in *Perpetuating the Family Business* that "the most successful business families I know invest a great amount of time and effort into learning communication skills, and they find it very, very powerful to learn these skills together." I could not have said it better.

Communicating with the next generation is critical. All children want to communicate with their parents, but too often parents do not listen; because they think they are wiser, they end up telling children how they should live their lives. I have never met a child who did not want to communicate with parents, as long as the child was given the opportunity to do so and would not be put down or criticized. When asking a question, it is wise to wait for a response; a short silence can be golden. This two-way communication should start as soon as a child can understand the purpose, and it must be done at a level where the child can comprehend. As children become older, it becomes even more important to discuss with them their ambitions. Without dictating to them, parents need to communicate their desires. For example, instead of saying, "You will go to college," a parent might say, "Have you considered which college you'd like to attend?" Use neutral language that does not telegraph your personal preference, or approval or disapproval of a given choice. Instead of pushing the child toward a profession, you might ask if the child has developed any interest in careers. Knowing their interests will help you direct them without appearing to be telling them what they must do.

One point worth noting: When a husband works and the wife stays home (or the other way around), the husband has spent eight to twelve hours communicating with adults, while the wife has spent the same time caring for the children and attending to the household chores. When the husband comes home, his first desire is to immediately speak with the children, but the wife desires to have adult conversation with her husband. This can present a built-in conflict unless the couple determines ahead of time how they will allocate time to make the children feel important and still converse together as adults. First, the father must be given some time to communicate with the children. The time for husband and wife to speak with each other, uninterrupted by children, should be clearly defined. It should be a quiet time, and its importance must not be minimized. If at all possible, both parents should attend the children's after-school activities together; the children then know and appreciate the parents' support, even though they may not express it verbally. If both spouses work, the same rules apply. Admittedly, at this time both parents want to speak with children, but both must also learn to communicate regularly with each other. Again, it is important to provide a structured environment in which the children's needs are attended to and the adults have time for conversation. Although I did not follow this practice, I understand from others that a particularly effective way to create time and space for adult conversation is for husband and wife to get away together for a day, maybe once a quarter, while leaving the children in someone else's care.

As children get older and reach post high school years, parents need to continue to listen to their concerns and issues. Children need a trustworthy and non-prejudicial sounding board for their concerns, even though discussions may not always be about pleasant issues. Often children communicate bad news indirectly. Parents might hear remarks such as "My professor just talks and does not listen to anyone," or "This isn't a good school—I think I should transfer," or "My boss gives me only menial assignments; maybe I should quit." All these comments relay an underlying message. It is important to listen without rebuttal; then at the appropriate time, ask, "What would you like to do?" Parents might put forth some suggestions for consideration, but they need to let the child decide upon the preferred plan of action. Generally, the child will come up with a suitable answer and feel comfortable about implementing it.

In our family, Rosemary and I considered ourselves facilitators for such conversations. We provided the environment for this kind of communication in several ways. As often as possible we had dinner together. At the dinner table we would pose a question and let the boys do the talking, and we would just listen. We also set aside a Saturday or Sunday each month, and let one of the boys choose an activity in which all of us would participate. This gave each child a sense of importance, and allowed each one to communicate his desires and interests.

Now that my sons have grown up and started families of their own, we continue communicating regularly with both our children and grandchildren. We take our entire extended family—our sons, their wives, and children—on a one-week family trip twice a year. Early on, we chose the destination with their interests in mind, but now that our children are grown, we let our sons and their families choose the destinations. Generally,

Skiing Steamboat on one of the early family trips. Front row: Chuck, Lori, J. David III, Mike. Back row: J. David II holding Owen, Jack, Rosemary.

since we travel together twice annually, we can accommodate everyone's wishes over a period of time. I highly recommend family trips such as these because bringing a family together in this way accomplishes four objectives:

1. It allows grandparents to see children and grandchildren together over some extended period of time, as opposed to the infrequent shorter visits of four or five hours on a weekend afternoon.

2. It permits grandparents to see all generations interacting. Clearly, there is a born-in rivalry among siblings but also a born-in pride in each other's accomplishments. This camaraderie can best be fostered if siblings and cousins are given an environment where they can interact among themselves. In a home environment there is not a significant block of time in which they can spend time with each other.

3. Trips can instill in children a "culture of travel and adventure." Going away encourages them to get out of

On a family excursion to Washington, D.C. Left to right: David, Michael, Jack, Purnima, Chuck, and Leon. *(Photo by Rosemary Gulati)*

their normal environment and have new experiences. Trips need not be expensive. Whether fifty miles or five thousand miles, the journeys will accomplish the objectives of bringing the family together, away from home and its everyday demands. While the cost of a trip must be within the family's means, the objectives remain the same.

4. Finally, during these outings the family should schedule structured meetings between parents and children with a written agenda and minutes that could form the basis for future meetings. Our family started these meetings when our sons were teenagers, and during our family trips Rosemary and I always set aside time to meet with our sons alone. The format for these meetings has been generally consistent. We discuss what is happening in their lives and share what is going on in ours. We ask them what they hope to accomplish in the next six months. In some of our trips we assign a book for them to read that we will all discuss when the family next gathers. One further tip: Parents should allow the children to do most of the talking at these family meetings and take minutes so everyone will know what topics to discuss when the family meets again.

If entrepreneurs desire to bring the next generation into the business, they need to educate their children about the business and any issues affecting it. They should seek input and ideas from the next generation; they may be surprised how much their heirs comprehend, and what ideas they put forth. By talking with young adults in this way, the entrepreneur forms a background that allows children to understand their father or mother and the business better. In the future, these talks can form the basis for the children to decide whether or not to join the business. Often a parent assumes that the child will succeed him or her in the business, only to discover that the child has no interest. Frequently, this situation occurs because parents did not take steps to bring the child along and develop in him or her some understanding of the business environment; what a missed opportunity for both generations. I felt fortunate that our three children decided to come into Fidelity Technologies and my other companies. They made that choice with the full knowledge of the challenges they would face, and with no guarantee of success.

As the children grow up and begin to have children of their own, it is critical to create some kind of homogenous unit among children and grandchildren. How often does one see a family where the cousins hardly ever see each other? In addition, brothers and sisters become further apart for no reason other than they are too busy with their own families and do not spend enough time to keep in close contact with each other. I felt it was my responsibility not only to see that my children grew up as a close-knit family but also to insure that my grandchildren had the same experience within our extended family. In our family, we fostered family togetherness in three ways:

1. Like all families we get together for special occasions— birthdays, baptisms, holidays and the like. Most families have these kinds of experiences. We certainly take advantage of occasions like these for family get-togethers, and I am happy that all of my sons live within of an hour of each other; therefore, they can all join in celebrations frequently.

2. I wanted to be certain that the grandchildren had other opportunities to gather in informal settings not limited to these special occasions. For that reason we scheduled the above mentioned twice-yearly family trips. These trips

also brought our daughters-in-law together to form closer relationships with each other as well as their brothers-in-law. At the same time, the cousins had great opportunities to get to know one another. Rosemary and I get a great amount of pleasure from seeing our grandchildren bond with each other. They play—and argue, too!—but over the years, the rivalries diminish. I know that, in time, they will form cohesive bonds and will include their cousins in their lives when they are adults.

3. As I grew closer to retirement, I began to think about how I could communicate directly with my grandchildren. I believe it is important to establish this cross-generational communication so grandchildren will learn directly about their grandparents' life experiences and values. I decided to write a letter to my grandchildren when each reached the age of twelve and could understand the thoughts I wanted to communicate. In these missives I communicate my values, moral standards, ethics, and desires for them. I try to keep my thoughts on a high level, but at the same time, avoid preaching. I started out writing monthly, but as topics narrowed, I moved to quarterly letters. *(Sample letters are included in Appendix B of this book.)*

I believe that it is also imperative that grandparents develop a one-on-one relationship with each individual grandchild, so that child and grandparent get to know each other better. Here, too, I decided to use excursions as a way of creating that bond. As each child reaches the age of twelve, Rosemary or I will take that child on an adventure trip —just the grandparent and grandchild—to a destination of the grandchild's choosing. I will take the boys; Rosemary will take the girls. We will schedule another similar trip as each grandchild completes high school.

In the event that we may not be alive or in good health when some of our younger grandchildren turn twelve or complete high school, we have worked out a plan with our sons and their wives to continue these mentoring trips. The oldest son and his wife will serve as "surrogate grandparents" for the children of the youngest son, the middle son and his wife will care for the children of the oldest son, and the youngest son and his wife will serve in this role for the children of the middle son.

I have developed several objectives for these excursion trips:

1. I encourage the child to pick an activity that they have never done and have an interest in doing. My oldest grandchild, when he turned twelve, wanted to learn fly fishing, so

Grandson David, age 12, on grandfather/grandson fly fishing trip to Idaho, 2008.

we went to Idaho where the fly fishing is known to be exceptional. My second grandson wanted to try trophy fishing, so we went to Cabo San Lucas in Mexico, renowned for striped marlin fishing.

Grandson Owen, age 12, reeling in a white marlin on grandfather/ grandson trip in Cabo San Lucas, Mexico, 2010.

2. I want each child to feel that this trip is uniquely his or her time. These trips are also very revealing to me, as I suspect they are for the child as well. He or she has a chance to be alone with a grandparent and be the center of attention in an environment of his or her choosing.

3. The greater bonus of the trip, however, is that it allows the child to open up to the grandparent in a way that does not happen in routine interaction. In my experience most children have the desire to communicate their

achievements with others, but rarely do they have a forum for doing so. During these get-away trips, I generally try to prompt discussion by inquiring how the child is doing in school, who is his best friend, what is his best and worst subject, and what are his ambitions? I also ask what his most exciting time was in school last year; did he have an argument with someone, and how did he resolve it? In addition, I inquire if he had a teacher who did not treat him as he thought he should have been treated. I'm also interested in knowing if he ever discovered afterward that something he blamed on the teacher was really his fault, and what does he want to be—a leader or a follower? I do not discuss these matters as an interrogation, but rather as a part of conversations at different moments throughout our trip.

Whenever you converse with a grandchild, it is important to let the child speak, remembering that the child needs more time than an adult to formulate his or her thoughts. Too often the adult speaks for the child, if only to fill in the void created by the silence. For me, these conversations have been very helpful in getting my grandchildren to open up to me, not only at our one-on-one outings, but also, thereafter. These discussions have provided me much insight into the child's thinking, and without being didactic, I can provide guidance that can help shape their thinking and decision-making.

One of the most effective ways to establish communications with the next generation is to find a topic of common interest. In our family, watching and playing sports has been a way to interact both as a unit and as individuals. We always encouraged our children to play sports, and they have participated to the level of their interest and abilities. Sports provide an avenue for discussion

On the golf course at Bonita Bay *(left to right)* Chuck, Mike, Jack, and Dave.

Participating in Phillies Phantasy Camp with sons. Left to right: Charles, Dave, Jack, Mike.

among people of otherwise divergent interests. There are no financial barriers—rich and poor can play or watch. In addition, sports form lifelong habits of exercise that promote health.

Not every family may be interested in sports. Some may find common interest in music, politics, art, or travel. The specific topic chosen as a means of establishing intergenerational communication and building bonds is not important. What is crucial, however, is that there is some activity that can draw the family together outside of narrow family interests. The family will look forward to gatherings when they can exchange the latest information on their topics of interest.

Making Major Purchases

In relating the story of my career, I described several deals in which I bought or sold companies. However, over the course of a lifetime, one makes many other major purchases—a home, an automobile, perhaps other real estate or substantial investments in coins, precious metals and the like. Being prepared to make such purchases can make a significant difference in your financial situation, prevent unnecessary expenditures that may drain your bank account, and even avoid disagreements among family members. I was fortunate that, early on, I realized that an automobile was a depreciating asset, but also a necessity in American life. When I purchased my first car in 1965, I had to take out a loan and make monthly payments. Once the car payments were no longer required, I continued to make similar payments at the same intervals to my own separate account, earmarked "next car fund." After three years I had sufficient funds to purchase the next car for cash. I continued to repeat this process, and that put me in a position to buy a new car every three to five years, should I choose to do so.

The key to buying any asset wisely begins with research. In 1978, I bought at auction ten acres of unimproved land in Chester County, Pennsylvania, borrowing $18,000 of the $24,000 purchase price. I first researched township ordinances and determined that the land could be subdivided. This knowledge assured me that the value of this land would increase. Sure enough, a year later I was able to sell this property for nearly $40,000, paying off my loan and retaining a tidy profit.

I have been fortunate, too, in purchasing vacation homes. As our children grew, Rosemary and I began discussing the possibility of buying a second home where we could take the family for vacations and holidays. I wanted a home in the mountains; she wanted a place at the New Jersey shore. Each offered different advantages. The boys were growing old enough to enjoy skiing, and of course, everyone enjoyed going to the beach. Rather than make a final decision on one or the other, we did extensive research on both types of properties. That way we would be ready to make a purchase when we found an opportunity that presented the best deal. We also began saving to purchase a property, once we identified the kind of second home we wanted.

As it turned out, in 1983 we purchased our mountain home first, at auction. We found a townhouse that we could afford on Camelback Mountain in the Poconos, in northeast Pennsylvania, just two hours' drive from our home. We were enthusiastic about our first vacation home, and visited there almost every weekend year round, most importantly during ski season. This ski-in and ski-out place was a dream-come-true for our boys, who could ski out directly from home, spend time on the slopes by themselves, and return right to the front door, where Rosemary would have hot chocolate waiting for them. Then one winter, when the boys were older, we took them to the Rocky Mountains to ski. Suddenly, the place in the Poconos lost its luster, and we began taking trips to various ski resorts in the Rockies every winter. Knowing that we wouldn't be using our home in the Poconos as much as we had in the past, we sold it.

However, since we never lost our interest in purchasing a beach property, we spent time getting smart about properties at the New Jersey shore. It was two hours east of our residence in Wayne, Pennsylvania. When we first began looking in the late 1980s, property was simply too expensive. Speculators were purchasing second homes with the intent to flip them. However, in 1990-91 the country suffered a recession in the housing market, and prices declined. We knew exactly what we wanted. We were insistent on getting waterfront property on navigational water—after all, as the saying goes, "they aren't making any more waterfronts"—so we knew that when the market recovered, these properties would appreciate first. We had scouted out several areas, and were ready to buy when a builder who had constructed twenty-four condo units in Avalon, NJ went bankrupt. The bank took possession of the property, and in 1995, when the bank auctioned these condos, we were able to get a choice condo at a good price.

Over the years, auctions have provided excellent opportunities for me to obtain properties at reasonable prices. Prior to the internet age, I routinely subscribed to a number of auction lists, so I received notifications when auctions were scheduled. When I saw an intriguing opportunity, I obtained additional information and conducted research on the property. This knowledge helped me set a rigid, maximum price that I was willing to bid. Adhering strictly to this price helped me avoid "auction fever." By participating in auctions, I was able to secure homes at below-market prices in Pennsylvania, New Jersey and Florida. I have also bought other items at auction, including

Home purchased at auction in 2001 in Oley PA. *(Photo by Leslie Leh)*

automobiles, boats, coins, and of course, Stokesay Castle, the property I had had my eye on for nearly two decades.

I am thankful for my successful purchases at auctions, but I am also thankful for what I did not get at a couple of auctions. There are lessons to be learned here, too. In 1977, without proper research, I bought some building lots in the Poconos at an auction. Fortunately, I had three days to retract this deal. Almost immediately I began to have serious reservations. After some additional research it became clear that these properties were not the right deal for us, so during the three day period I rescinded the purchase. Years later, in 2009, I looked at a 301-acre tract of land in Florida that had been confiscated by the government and was being put up for auction by the U.S. Treasury. I visited the property, spoke with numerous people, searched all the court and county records, and evaluated the prices of recent similar property sales; in short I did thorough research. The property, not far from the beach, appeared to have potential for a future housing development. I estimated that it was worth $2.1 million. I signed up to participate in the online auction, where I was able to bid from the comfortable surroundings of my office. Frankly, I succumbed to "auction fever" and ended up being the high bidder at $4.3 million, and I was now stuck with a purchase price of twice as much as I knew the property was worth. I had a sinking feeling in the pit of my stomach.

However, as I like to tell family and friends, "my mother came to the rescue"—that is, by some form of Divine Providence—I ended up being saved from my rash action. As with all transactions of this type involving the government, this deal was subject to review before the bid would be accepted and the sale deemed final. Luckily for me, the government rejected my bid. I have no idea why; I can only assume that my mother above was looking out for me. When word got out that I had lost the property, two other bidders called to tell me that I should thank my lucky stars that the deal had fallen through. Looking back, I can see how right these people were. I had no specific plans for this property when I bid on it. I would have been forced to sit on it while I figured out what to do, in the meantime incurring all sorts of expenses on an asset that was bringing me no return. Developing this large property would have been problematic also, as getting permission in Florida to create new subdivisions is very difficult, and neighbors frequently fight tooth-and-nail to prevent further growth in their area. Furthermore, this tract sat between two modular home subdivisions; there would have been little opportunity to create an upscale neighborhood. In short, I had ignored my own pre-auction parameters of price and purpose. For a disciplined person like me, it was a serious error in judgment.

Another venture that did not end successfully was my attempt to purchase a new financial services product being offered at auction. Insurance policies that had been bundled were being sold in a fashion similar to mortgage-backed securities. In this case, the policies were written on people afflicted with HIV. I saw an advertisement in the New York Times that the government had confiscated and was auctioning a number of pooled insurance policies. The government guaranteed that the policies were valid and up-to-date, so I thought I would investigate this business to see if it might be profitable. I learned that it was, indeed, possible to make money on these policies, so I decided to enter the auction. In these auctions the government first identifies someone to act as a "stalking horse." This person puts in a bid for the lot, thus setting the minimum price for the auction. Other bidders must bid a certain amount over this initial bid, and the stalking horse has the right to match the price and buy the policies. I bid on some of these offerings, but the stalking horse always matched my bid. In this case, I was unsuccessful in obtaining what I wanted to purchase, but I did not exceed what I thought was an acceptable risk, so I was not unhappy to be outbid.

Before the advent of the internet, most auctions were conducted on-site or at a government facility, so it was easier to succeed and take acceptable risks. Most people at those earlier auctions were serious bidders who, like me, had done some homework to know what an item was worth. On rare occasions, however, a bidder would drop in on a whim and get caught up in "auction fever," driving the price of an item far above its value. Online bidding has made the process more complicated, because it is no longer possible to observe the other bidders to distinguish between those who are serious and have done their research and those who, to put it bluntly, have more money than brains. Once bidding begins, bidders often bid up the price in small increments, but these small amounts add up quickly. If not careful, bidders can find that they have exceeded the maximum intended bid. During an auction it is imperative to remain calm and participate only as long as the bid does not exceed your pre-determined amount. Do not allow yourself to be swayed by peer pressure.

I can sum up my advice about making purchases this way: Entrepreneurs must start by identifying true needs versus emotional desires; they must then perform detailed research, and not become captivated by a particular piece of property, business, or deal, nor chase after the latest fad. A significant portion of the research may never result in a successful transaction, but the point of the research is to identify good and bad deals, and act accordingly. The entrepreneur will have gained considerable experience and knowledge that may transfer to future deals, and he/she may be more ready to take advantage of future opportunities as they arise.

Getting Involved in Politics and Professional Activities

I have observed that most entrepreneurs consider it important to participate in civic and political activities. They keep informed about what is happening locally, regionally and nationally. Perhaps they volunteer at a local charity, civic or political organization, church, or industry association. Usually they register to vote, and perhaps contribute to causes in which they believe. In 1973, I registered as a Democrat and made contributions to the Democratic Party at the local and national levels. I believed it was important to take an active role in civic and political activities. My experiences in these areas may serve as a cautionary tale to entrepreneurs who are attracted to public service.

By 1975, I had remarried and was established in my community outside Philadelphia. In that year, I decided to enter politics. By this time my political inclinations had become more conservative, so I changed my registration to Republican and put myself forward as a candidate, and was elected as Republican Committeeman from my district in Upper Merion Township.

When Pennsylvania was established as a Commonwealth, townships were the original subdivisions of counties in Pennsylvania. Later, cities and boroughs were formed from land originally included within a township. Like all municipal governments, townships provided a variety of services to citizens including fire and police protection, sewer and water, as well as parks and recreation. In addition, townships set up and enforced zoning and development ordinances. Therefore, serving in Township government was a way to become directly involved in community improvement. I found the work exhilarating.

In 1979, I was still trying to make a go of the Fidelity Investment Builder Model Home Buy and Lease-Back Program, while working full-time as Vice President of Marketing for General Data Systems. I normally worked in my Philadelphia office on Mondays, and then traveled from Tuesday through Friday for business. The Upper Merion Township Board of Supervisors met on Monday evenings; since I had Monday evenings free, I decided to run for a position on the Board of Supervisors. Rosemary cautioned me that if I were elected, my Monday evenings would also be tied up, but I still decided to run. I teamed up with Abe Martin, another candidate, for two seats on the Board of Supervisors, and we campaigned as a team. Abe was well known in the community, as he and his firm had been township engineers for decades. His reputation gave us name recognition with voters, while I did much of the legwork. I knocked on most of the doors in the township and handled the publicity. We won both seats. We were not the endorsed nominees of the Upper Merion Republican Committee; and my decision to run as an independent candidate against the Party's anointed candidate would come back to haunt me later.

I was sworn into office in January 1980. Soon after my election as township supervisor it became clear that the job required serving numerous self-interest groups, many with petty issues. Abe Martin and I decided that we would not go along with the "business as usual" approach to handling Township matters. We were branded as mavericks because we would not rubberstamp the directives of the political machine in the township or the county. We were two of five supervisors, so we were often outvoted by the others.

Photo used in political literature when running for U.S. Congress in 1982.

Despite being in the minority on many issues at Township Supervisors' meetings, I came to believe that I might be able to serve a greater constituency. Convinced that I had the necessary qualifications to represent people in my area, in 1982 I decided to run in the Republican primary for the U.S. Congress against a six-term incumbent who had never before faced a challenge in the primary. I did not have Party support or the resources necessary to defeat such a formidable opponent. Equally important, I did not totally understand how the political system worked. I thought voters would look at candidates' records and vote for the best candidate. However, in Montgomery County, the bulk of this particular Congressional District, the Republican Committee, a powerful machine at that time, anointed a slate of candidates. One reporter wrote that, instead of examining the candidates' credentials, nearly a quarter million registered Republican voters would faithfully trudge to the polls and vote the Party line. At that time Montgomery County was a Republican bastion, so a win in the Republican primary virtually guaranteed a victory in the general election.

I lost the election but felt good for having made the effort. I was the first opposition candidate to run an independent, computerized Congressional District campaign, which we did from Rosemary's dining room. A steady stream of friends, neighbors, and constituents stepped up to support me. In the end I discovered that running for Congress required incredible organization and money. I was working fulltime while trying to run my own campaign; I did not have any paid staff. I suspect my effectiveness at work suffered as a result. I eventually came to the realization that, at this level, being a politician is a full-time job. If I were to run for national office again, I would certainly do things differently: I would make politics my sole profession. From 1982-85, I devoted my energies to the responsibilities of being a township supervisor and tended to the needs of my constituents. During this time, my colleagues elected me Chairman of the Board of Supervisors. In 1985 I ran for reelection, but was defeated. This time, the party came after me to get revenge for having run against a fourteen-year incumbent in the 1982 Congressional primary election. One powerful county leader told me that the vendetta was not against me personally, but the Montgomery County Republican Party wanted to set an example for anyone else who might challenge their authority in the future. Although I left the political arena when my term as Township Supervisor expired in January 1986, my sojourn into political life taught me some valuable lessons. I discovered that business and family suffer from this kind of involvement. Local participation is possible part-time, but if one has state or national ambitions, then full-time participation and money is required. I found that I could be more effective supporting politicians whose positions on the issues were aligned with mine. Now my family and I support the political process from behind the scenes rather than as active participants.

My foray into politics was followed by a stint as a business executive on the national stage. Sometime during the mid-1980s, at roughly the same time I became president of Viatek, I began a long involvement with several regional and national organizations that promoted the interests of small businesses. On the national level, I was privileged to serve as a delegate to the 1986 White House Conference on Small Business, accompanying seventy-four other Pennsylvania business executives to what was described as the first national conference in six years devoted exclusively to the special problems of small businesses. I was particularly proud to have been selected; my election showed that my peers respected me. During the next Republican administration, I was asked by President George H.W. Bush to serve on the Small Business Advisory Committee of the Federal Communications Commission. At one time or another I was active in the Chamber of Commerce, various state organizations, and the National Federation of Independent Business, an affiliation I maintained until the year 2000. My work on the national level took me as far as Africa, where in 1992 I was part of a delegation advising countries on matters involving the transition from military to civil rule. The conference was held in Dakar, Senegal under the auspices of Senegal's Minister of State, Abdoulaye Wade. Forty-two African heads of state and their opposition leaders attended.

Stan Straughter, a Philadelphia businessman, and I were the two delegates representing the United States. I had the good fortune to become personally acquainted with Minister Wade, and we remained friends for many years. Eventually he served as President of Senegal from 2000-2012.

In 1994, Abdoulaye came to America to seek support for his initiatives in Africa. He requested that Stan Straughter and I

Jack on airplane in Africa with Abdoulaye Wade, Minister of State of Senegal, later to become Senegal's president.

accompany him to Philadelphia, Washington, D.C. and Boston. During his stop in Philadelphia we arranged for him to meet the mayor, as well as political and civic leaders. Rosemary and I then entertained him in our home for dinner. He arrived with two security agents toting Uzi submachine guns—a surprise to us, to say the least. We expected his security agents to dine with us in the dining room, but Abdoulaye insisted that they follow protocol and eat separately in the kitchen.

In Washington, we arranged for Minister Wade to give a speech at the National Press Club. It was broadcast by many international radio stations and publicized in the press. We also organized a meeting with the Congressional Black Caucus. We then flew from Washington to Boston. The trip itself was uneventful, but months later the FBI met with me about the trip, pointing out that Uzis had been carried on the plane, which was clearly against regulations. However, the trip had been approved by the Department of State, and nothing came of the investigation.

Late in the 1990s, however, I began to question myself about my time-consuming involvement in extracurricular activities. Was I getting a swelled head over the honors being accorded me? And what was this time commitment costing? A candid analysis told me that I was spending too little time on my own businesses that were no longer "mom and pop" operations, but multi-national companies with hundreds of employees. I was not in businesses that allowed me to capitalize on the contacts I was making in order to enhance my "bottom line." Instead, I was taking time away from my businesses and my family, and receiving no monetary benefit. Once I took stock of how I was spending my time, I cut out virtually all these extra activities, and focused once again on Fidelity Technologies and the European companies I was managing at the time.

Lessons Learned: *The great lesson here is simple but profound: An entrepreneur must set correct priorities and stick to them. One has only so much time. I do not want to suggest that* *politics or professional organizations are unimportant. On the contrary, they play a vital role in shaping the business climate in America. But the individual entrepreneur must exercise caution before getting directly involved in these activities. It is fine to devote time and energy to associations and political causes once time allows, but an entrepreneur must stay focused on what is important, or business and family will suffer.*

Planning Your Finances

Once you have accumulated some wealth, what do you do with it? This is a question that too many people fail to ask early in their careers, but it is one that bears serious attention.

Once you have accumulated even a modest sum of money, you need to find the best way to invest it. As a young person, you may have taken some risks with finances, knowing that you would have time to recoup losses if the investments in the market or in a business did not pan out. However, as you grow older, the appetite to take risks should diminish, and more attention paid to capital preservation. Therefore, it becomes critically important to know how to invest funds wisely.

After meeting with roughly two dozen financial planners, it became clear to me that the majority of them had great ideas for either money management or life insurance products, but they were full of "book learning," and not first-hand experience. The best way I know to safeguard money and still see growth is to invest regularly in equity and bond mutual funds in proportion to one's tolerance for risk. You should not chase high returns available during good times, but instead should pursue a strategy of reasonable returns over a long period. Once the investment strategy is set, learn to stay the course, even in tough times, because significant market returns are realized early in a market recovery, and if you sell in down times, you will most likely miss the "bump" when the market recovers. Unless you have strong investment skills, in my opinion, it is best to retain a professional advisor who is reasonable, who provides consistent advice and is not swayed by the latest fads of the day. It is important to meet with the advisor regularly, stay abreast of one's investment portfolio, and adjust as personal needs change.

Life Insurance also should be an integral part of your financial planning. It is important to purchase life insurance policies to protect the family and the business in the event of an unseen catastrophe that could lead to the loss of lifestyle and business. I have always been a strong believer in having this security blanket that provides the family the necessary resources to stay in the family home and take care of daily expenses. Some people believe only those with substantial assets or a high income need life insurance; nothing could be farther from the truth. Everyone needs to plan for the unexpected so that families can maintain their standard of living if something happens to the principal breadwinner.

Once a small or large nest egg has been accumulated, an entrepreneur has an obligation to set up estate planning for the following reasons:

1. Estate planning helps minimize tax obligations. Of course, you must comply with the law, but as Justice John Paul Stevens once said, "No citizen is obligated to pay the government any more than he is required." In addition,

estate planning helps to identify income sources and spending habits for the years going forward. Thorough planning also identifies financial strengths and weaknesses, making it possible to take corrective action as necessary.

2. A good plan communicates to your family your wishes for your estate when you die. Therefore, good estate planning can minimize, if not eliminate, any in-fighting that might occur among family members.

3. Planning can mitigate the helpless feeling that comes to a grieving family who may have no idea where important papers are kept or your burial desires. Most importantly, a good plan helps inform heirs, especially children, what their role will be in settling your affairs.

4. If there are reasons to split your inheritance in a formula that does not provide equal shares to each child, the siblings must know up front the formula you have developed, and why, to minimize the idea that one child is favored. For example, one may have a child with a disability and may choose to leave more resources for the care of this child, and when the child's expenses have been paid, divide the remainder among the others As long as the siblings know, even though they may not agree, hopefully they will understand. Finally, if the will is explained to the children before you pass on, it will be much easier for them to understand your intentions.

Of course, one need not wait to pass on a portion of an estate to heirs. If the children are responsible and use money wisely, one may want to give them tax-free gifts. Government tax policy promotes a certain amount of giving without tax consequences for either party. For example, in 2012, each individual is allowed a $5 million lifetime gift-tax exemption; for those who are married, the total becomes $10 million. In addition to this lifetime gift tax exemption, at the present time, you can make annual gifts of up to $13,000 to anyone under the so-called tax-free-gift rule. This gift will not trigger any federal gift taxes for the donor or the recipient, nor will it reduce the federal lifetime gift-tax or estate-tax exemptions. The benefits of making tax-free gifts are twofold: each gift reduces one's taxable estate, and the taxes on future earnings on such gifts now shift to the recipient who may be taxed at a lower rate. This strategy works particularly well for those who wait until late in life to start serious estate planning. The tax laws are complex and change often; therefore, a thorough action plan is a must. It is mandatory to consult with competent professionals (accountant, lawyer, and financial planner) who specialize in estate planning.

For younger children or grandchildren, the tax code provides for college savings plans known as 529 Plans that are available in states across America and offer significant tax advantages. These plans are funded with after-tax dollars, but the earnings accumulate tax-free as long as the funds are used for education, and the plan defines education very broadly and offers significant flexibility. Tax laws can change, of course, and there is no guarantee that this option will be available in the future. However, it makes sense to speak with tax and financial professionals versed in these matters to discuss available options. A key point to be made here is that one does not have to be wealthy to take advantage of these programs. Small gifts or modest deposits made regularly into 529 college accounts are excellent ways to accumulate funds for future education while both generations are still alive.

Planning for the Future of Your Business

How often have you driven by a store where you once shopped only to find its doors bolted and a CLOSED sign in the window? How often have you discovered that the family-owned retail establishment or a parts supplier has gone out of business because the owner decided to retire and could not find anyone to take over the business? Sadly, this happens too often in America. It is usually the result of poor planning on the part of entrepreneurs, who have spent most of their time starting a business and keeping it running, but who have not devoted sufficient attention to the future of the business, that is, …succession planning.

In Part III of this book I described the steps I took at Fidelity Technologies to prepare my sons to become owners of the company. I also, discussed the process I took in 2011, as I approached age 70, to gift my companies to my three sons. I am a strong believer in transferring ownership of one's business to the next generation. In fact, when children show interest in the family business, it should be the owner's responsibility to help them prepare to take over. There is no "one size fits all" solution in succession planning, but one thing is clear: if you don't do it, circumstances will do it for you. Clearly, any method chosen must be done carefully and in concert with your attorneys, accountants, and financial advisors.

Most likely, your business is your most valuable asset. To insure a smooth transition of ownership, the transfer should be planned and executed in an orderly manner, and there are no short cuts. Expect this planning and execution period to last from four to seven years. The plan you choose should be structured to reflect your true desires and needs and should be designed to minimize income taxes as well as gift and estate taxes. After all, what really matters is the amount of money you keep.

I believe it is best to begin with three basic questions:

1. Is it more advantageous to sell or gift the business?
2. Will transfer of ownership be to a third party, partners or employees, venture capitalists, or family members?
3. Will the transfer of the business take place during your lifetime or at your death?

Each option has its advantages and disadvantages. If your business has been successful and you decide to sell it, you must retain a merger and acquisition specialist, who is in the best position to promote the sale in such a way that will provide for maximum exposure to potential buyers and still maintain the confidentiality of the process.

Possibly the simplest way to transfer ownership is to sell the business outright. Such a sale also provides the greatest flexibility in determining both the timing and conditions of sale. An outright sale can be made at any time: before retirement, as part of a planned retirement, after retirement, or upon death. If you decide to sell your business as part of a retirement strategy, the proceeds can help maintain your lifestyle. If the sale is finalized upon your death, the proceeds can be used for the care of the surviving family or to pay estate taxes and other final expenses.

Selling To A Third Party

In cases where an entrepreneur has no children or close relatives who possess either the qualifications or the interest in the business, there are several options, and each should be considered carefully, again always in concert with professional advisors. Some options allow the owner's continued involvement in its operations; others permit a walk-away when the transaction is completed, or shortly thereafter.

One such option is to issue stock and become a publicly traded company, especially if the business is sufficiently large and needs an infusion of capital to expand operations. However, in most cases the initial public offering does not provide a significant opportunity for the owners to cash out. I would caution that unless your company has upwards of $100 million in annual revenues, and is profitable, it most likely makes no sense to go public. Going public requires significant time and may cause disruptions in the everyday tasks of running the business. In addition, there are substantial initial costs to such an undertaking. A public company must comply, at significant cost, with monumental, additional, regulatory requirements imposed by local, state, and federal governments. If your company is not sufficiently large, it may not attract interest from the investment community, and you may have difficulty finding a stock analyst willing to write about your company. Reports from these analysts generate interest among investors and optimize the opportunities for secondary offerings that usually provide the best avenues for owners to cash out. Finally, a publicly traded company will change the way you do business. You must report to a board of directors. The company will be required to file quarterly and yearly detailed financial results, and all other major events must be disclosed almost immediately. No longer will you be able to take the long view toward success; you will be held accountable for short-term performance, often at the expense of long-term growth and stability.

Every so often an entrepreneur may be enticed to take a less expensive and faster route to become publicly traded by using a reverse merger whereby a profitable and growing business is merged with a penny stock publicly-traded shell company. Business owners must be especially wary of such enticements. Penny stocks are common shares of small public companies that trade at less than one dollar. These shell companies usually have little or no hard assets, and may have been unprofitable over a significant period of time. Penny stocks are considered to be highly speculative and high risk investments, but they may still have a large potential for profit. As these penny stocks do not meet the requirements of the major stock exchanges such as the New York, American, or NASDAQ, they are often traded on the Over-The-Counter (OTC) Bulletin Board or Pink Sheets. Getting real-time share prices and selling your shares on these Boards can be difficult.

In addition, the business owner must be beware of the "roll over" option where one company may purchase a number of companies with stocks that have not been fully registered with the U.S. Securities and Exchange Commission in the hope of someday creating a critical mass that results in a public offering. If such an anticipated public offering is successful, the entrepreneur will be able to sell his shares on the open market.

For all these reasons, it makes sense to take a company public only if the need for cash outweighs all the concerns outlined above. Nevertheless, going public remains a viable alternative, but only after a detailed review of all options and careful consultation with professional advisors.

Another viable option is to sell your business to a competitor. A competitor will most likely offer the best deal because someone in the same business understands your company and will receive the most benefit from the combined entity. The transaction can be done cleanly if you take the time to draft appropriate documents spelling out all the terms of the sale. If you negotiate a cash transaction and receive full payment of the agreed-upon price at closing, you can walk away without any further responsibilities. However, in most cases the buyer will require significant warranties and representations, and will hold back 10 to 20 percent of the purchase price for a certain number of years as a security that all of the warranties and representations are correct. Buyers frequently find reasons to retain the money they have held back, ultimately making the sale less profitable for the seller, so when making the decision on fair market value of your company, you should be aware that there is a high probability that you will not get all of the held-back monies.

Another option is to merge your business with a competitor of similar size. I mention size specifically because in the event that you merge with a decidedly larger firm, the likelihood is that your business will simply be subsumed and your specific legacy obliterated (unless you plan to take your cash and run). Merging with a firm of equal size allows you to launch the joint venture as a substantial partner. Finding the right firm with which to merge is not easy. In addition to the financial considerations, you must make certain that the management philosophies of the companies coalesce, owners' personalities are compatible, and the vision for the new company is clearly defined. Merging your company is similar to bringing in a partner. After my experience at Viatek, I have resisted having partners because I valued operating independently. On the other hand, I realize that sometimes it may be necessary to bring in one or more partners in order to provide for certain additional financial, technical, or management resources. Partners can also be brought in as part of an exit strategy that calls for them to buy the business eventually.

Whatever option you choose, getting to the point of selling the business can pose some potential problems. As part of due diligence the potential buyer will require disclosure of significant confidential information. However, if the sale does not go through, you could find yourself at a competitive disadvantage, as your rival now knows your trade secrets, even with confidentiality and non-disclosure agreements in place. Therefore, it is of utmost importance that both parties sign a letter of intent outlining the significant terms of the sale before detailed information is exchanged. Even after the signing of a letter of intent, the seller should still be cautious about disclosing highly confidential data until both parties have agreed to all the significant terms of the sale and are ready to sign the final buy-sell agreement.

Selling to Partners or Employees

If you have one or more partners, you should consider transferring your shares of the business through a buy-sell agreement. This legally binding contract establishes the terms under which you will sell your interest in the business; it names potential purchasers, fixes the time of sale, and establishes a method for determining the price and payment terms. Having a buy-sell agreement can be a real boon for the business as it can avoid problems such as disrupted operations, dissolution, or liquidation should you become unable to continue operating the business through illness or death. The agreement also minimizes the chance that your business will be transferred to outsiders.

A buy-sell agreement also has benefits for your heirs. Being able to fix the purchase price of your shares can be especially helpful in estate planning. Because the purchase price is already fixed in the agreement, there's less chance of your heirs being treated unfairly. Ordinarily, funding for the buyout is arranged when the buy-sell agreement is executed. This means funds will be readily available to provide your estate with the liquidity that may be needed to settle expenses and pay estate taxes. Often these agreements are funded through insurance policies or by making regular payments to a specific account designated for this purpose.

Selling the business to employees may be more palatable if you wish to assure that the business continues to operate after you walk away. Selling to employees has the potential to preserve the culture you created, and is more likely to mean that those who worked for you will remain with the company. There are no guarantees, however; once the employees own the business, they are free to act in the same way as if you sold the business to a competitor or another outside party.

There are two options for passing on a business to employees. One is for a group to pool resources and buy your shares. Often, however, it is not possible for them to come up with funds to buy you out completely unless you offer them a long-term payment plan. Another method is for you to create an Employee Stock Ownership Plan (ESOP) whereby your employees become owners by holding stock in the company. This approach works well if you want to raise cash and have your employees invested directly in the work they are doing, while you remain with the company as principal owner and chief executive. The advantage for the employees is that the more profits the company generates, the greater will be their share value. As an alternative, you can sell all the company stock to employees and allow the new owners to select their own management team. Transferring your company to employees by means of an ESOP deserves serious investigation by any entrepreneur wishing to exit the business. However, anyone planning to pursue this option would do well to consult an ESOP expert before proceeding.

Selling to Venture Capitalists

If you anticipate selling to a third party, one more option to consider is to involve venture capitalists in your company. This option may provide an excellent way to get extra capital for your business while you continue to be directly involved in running it. However, the move to bring in venture capitalists comes with significant strings attached. Typically venture capitalists demand high rates of return on their investments, often in the range of 25 to 35 percent per year. Most have only a short-term interest in your business; they stay invested for five to seven years, but they have an exit strategy that allows them to pull out their money when they feel they have gotten all they can from their investment. Because they invest heavily in your operations, they expect results, and many will not hesitate to tell you how you should manage the business to achieve those results, and they are unmerciful in demanding that business plan objectives continuously be met. On the other hand, venture capitalists often can provide other resources and contacts, so it is possible that you may benefit from their expertise. The most important point I can emphasize is that both parties must be clear up front about mutual expectations.

Selling To Family

If you decide to transfer the business to your children, you need to answer the following questions:

1. Do you want to sell the business to your children at fair market value?
2. Are you in a financial position to gift the business to your children?

If you decide to sell the business at fair market value, the children may acquire the business through a purchase and sale agreement. Often children may not have sufficient funds available to buy the business outright, and they may not be able to get financing on their own. In such an event you may consider offering payment terms. For example, you may arrange for a buyout period over several years during which you retain the option to take back the business if the agreed-upon payments are not received. Care must be taken to set the payments so that they can be made from the cash flow of the business, and not create an unnecessary burden that may cause the business to eventually fail. Also keep in mind that children need cash flow for their own personal living expenses. During this period the children have free rein to run the business as they see fit, providing regular financial and other reports that you think are necessary to demonstrate the continuing viability of the business. Whether an entrepreneur sells the business outright to his children or arranges for them to purchase it on terms, it is best to do an arm's length transaction similar to one that would be arranged with someone outside the family; doing so keeps the focus on the business as a business and reminds everyone of the true value of the asset being transferred.

Another way to structure the transfer of a business to children is through the use of a private annuity. Under this arrangement the children promise to make periodic payments for the remainder of your life, or the life of your spouse or other person you may designate. Because this form of transfer is still considered a sale and not a gift, the transfer of ownership removes the business from your estate without creating any liability for gift or estate taxes. You are still liable for capital gains taxes, however, and the law has changed recently to eliminate the tax advantage you previously might have realized by spreading out these gains over time. Hence, it is always best to work closely with a tax professional before deciding to transfer your business through this mechanism.

Rather than using an annuity, you may find it more advantageous to transfer ownership by means of a self-canceling installment note (SCIN). Under the terms of a SCIN, the children execute a promissory note which obligates them to make a series of payments over time. However, should you die before payments have been completed, the remaining payments are canceled. The advantages to the children are obvious, but there are reasons for you to consider this option as well. A SCIN provides a lifetime income stream and allows you to avoid gift and estate taxes. At the same time, you retain a security interest in the business even though ownership has transferred.

You may also consider passing on the business as a gift. Ignoring, for a moment, the tax implications of this gesture, it might be wise to consider both the financial ramifications to the older generation and the psychological impact to the younger generation. For the entrepreneur who started and built a successful business, giving it to the next generation with no strings attached may seem like a generous way to assure their children's financial future. This strategy may work for you if you have sufficient assets outside the business that will allow you to retire comfortably. On the other hand, for most owners their business is their greatest asset, and they simply cannot afford to let it go without compensation. In addition, the recipients may have no sense of the value of the asset they are receiving. Consequently, those who take over may not feel it necessary to devote the same energy to maintain and grow the business.

There are other options as well. For example, rather than making an outright gift, you might establish a trust. You may stipulate that, under the terms of the trust, you may keep control of the business for as long as you want. You can decide to make the trust revocable which allows you to change your mind and terminate the trust at any time. In some cases, if the trust is structured correctly, placing your business in a revocable trust may allow your family to avoid probate for that portion of your estate when you die. Alternatively, you can set up an irrevocable trust that can provide you with income for a specified period of time and move your business out of your estate at a discounted tax rate. The drawback to the irrevocable trust is that once it is set up, it cannot be changed.

You can also transfer your interest to other family members through a family limited partnership (FLP). Under terms of a FLP you (and your spouse, if you choose) can be the general partners in the partnership. You retain control of the business and continue to receive income. Your children or other family members become limited partners. Once the business ownership has been transferred to the FLP, you may be able to substantially reduce the value of the business for tax purposes by making annual tax-free gifts to those family members who are limited partners.

A final note: Once you have decided what you will do, it is important to communicate your intentions. In my case, when I finally stepped away from my businesses to move into full retirement, I announced my plans to my employees and colleagues who have worked with me through the years, letting them know my decision, and expressing confidence in my sons to carry on and grow the businesses I had started or acquired. *A copy of each retirement letter is included in this book as Appendix C.*

Giving Back

In 2010, Chestnut Hill College, Rosemary's alma mater, approached us to contribute to the creation of a student complex to house a fitness center and student lounge. When dedicated

Jack *(left)* and Rosemary *(right)* with Carol Jean Vale SSJ *(center)*, President of Chestnut Hill College, at the dedication of the Jack and Rosemary Murphy Gulati Complex, 2012. *(Photo by Linda Johnson for Chestnut Hill College)*

in 2012, it was named the Jack and Rosemary Murphy Gulati '61 Complex. Confident that the institution had a sound plan and the new facility would serve a real purpose, we agreed to donate $1 million dollars as the lead gift for this project. Why we did so and how we arranged for this gift provides insight into my philosophy of "giving back" and offers some suggestions that successful entrepreneurs might find helpful in establishing their own mechanisms for sharing their good fortune with their communities.

My mother instilled in me the idea that one should contribute to those less fortunate or to organizations that serve worthy purposes. After my father died, she had little money of her own, but she always made it a point to support causes in which she believed. Even though she lived on Social Security for most of her life after 1967, she made annual contributions of $500 each to the Salvation Army and the American Red Cross. Perhaps even more remarkably, in 1978 she donated $5,000, most likely her life's savings, to the Joseph P. Kennedy Jr. Foundation to support Special Olympics. The Special Olympics was in its tenth year and had just initiated a Winter Olympics program. Why my mother chose to make such a generous donation was never clear to me. Perhaps she saw the Special Olympics as a program similar to ones that provided support to my brother Davinder. I had the pleasure of serving as go-between, forwarding the check and a letter from my mother to the Foundation. As a result, I received copies of the reply sent to my mother by Eunice Kennedy Shriver, in which Mrs. Shriver extended her personal thanks for the gift. Despite its affiliation with the Kennedy family, the Foundation was not large in 1978; my mother's contribution was indeed a notable one and prompted Mrs. Shriver to invite her to the next Olympics. My mother could not attend, but she was immensely pleased that her gift was making a difference for young men and women with disabilities.

The Joseph P. Kennedy, Jr. Foundation

1701 K STREET, NORTHWEST, SUITE 205
WASHINGTON, D. C. 20006
(202) 331-1731

February 7, 1979

Mrs. Leela W. Gulati
601 W. 113th Street
New York, NY   10025

Dear Mrs. Gulati:

I am overjoyed with your extremely generous contribution to
the Joseph P. Kennedy, Jr. Foundation. It is not often that
people offer on their own such large amounts. And, since the
Kennedy Foundation is not an extremely large foundation, $5,000
is very meaningful to us. I can assure you that the entire amount
will be used directly to help mentally retarded individuals
through our Special Olympics program, which I believe General
Montague described to your son.

I have attached some information about Special Olympics
which may interest you. I know that our Special Olympics organization in New York will be delighted to have you as a guest at a
Special Olympics event there. The largest event this year will be
the New York State Special Olympics at St. Bonaventure College on
June 8-10. The 1979 International Summer Special Olympics Games
will also be held in New York State at the State University College
of New York at Brockport on August 8-13. I would be delighted
to have you visit this exciting event.

On behalf of the Joseph P. Kennedy, Jr. Foundation and my
family, I sincerely thank you and your son for your marvelous
support.

Sincerely,

Eunice Kennedy Shriver

EKS/crg

Enclosures

Letter written by Eunice Kennedy Shriver thanking Leela Gulati for her major gift to the Special Olympics.

My mother also expressed her generosity to people in her homeland. Sometime after the great migration of Hindus from the Punjab into India, the government set aside an area in New Delhi for former refugees. Within this Gujranwala Section of the city, refugees from my home town were offered building lots at very reasonable prices. Even though my family had immigrated to the United States, my mother arranged for a two-story home with two apartments to be built on her property; my uncle Banarsi Dass Sethi in New Delhi supervised the construction. Originally, she had planned to move back to India, live in one apartment and rent the second. She intended to donate the rent money to the poor. But when she realized her health would not permit the move, she asked my uncle to rent both apartments and donate the rent money to support the poor.

Two-story house in Gujranwala Town, New Delhi, built by Jack's mother on land provided by the Indian government. Looking up at house are Jack (right) and cousin Harsh Sethi (left) in 1988.

With such a model for inspiration, it is small wonder that I decided that, when I was able, I would also give back to my community. Over the years Rosemary and I have supported charities, educational institutions, and political causes in which we believed. In 2002, however, we decided to formalize our gift-giving to charities and non-profits by establishing The Gulati Family Foundation. We began our Foundation with a $1,000 contribution and have added to it steadily. Sometimes we made contributions in cash, and sometimes in appreciated securities that provided a tax advantage to us. On occasion, those contributions have been substantial, such as the ones I made after selling the Chadderton Airport property, Fidelity Technologies, and the TeleAlarm Group. In 2010, a stock in which I had invested appreciated significantly. We transferred the stock to the Foundation and were thus able to have available the funds necessary to make the major gift to Chestnut Hill College.

Why establish a foundation? First, doing so gets one in the habit of giving. Money placed in the Foundation cannot be withdrawn for personal use. The principal may be left intact or distributed to worthy causes, but gifts can be made only to recognized charities and nonprofits. Additionally, current law requires that a foundation distribute a minimum of 5 percent of its net worth each year, although this figure is calculated over a two-year period to allow for fluctuations in the market that can affect the value of the foundation's investments. Hence, once one has set aside money in a foundation, one is required to give it away.

Another important reason we decided to start a family foundation was to leave a legacy for our children. We wanted them, too, to learn the importance of giving back, and we thought that participating in the foundation's activities would help them see how they might do so. We created a Foundation Board consisting of Rosemary and me, our three sons and their spouses. This board meets regularly to consider written requests for assistance from family members or from organizations. Recently our grandson David, age fifteen, approached the foundation for a donation to what he thought was a particularly worthy cause. A close friend had died from a rare form of cancer; David had served as a pallbearer at the funeral. The friend's family was establishing a foundation to support cancer research. We were thrilled that David had seen fit to ask for this gift because it indicated to us that our idea of using the foundation to support worthy causes had already taken root in the next generation.

When we first started the foundation, we wanted to contribute to organizations in which our family members had some connection. But we also understood that we would support other causes as well. Hence, we were able to assist the Easter Seals group when its camp flooded, threatening the opening of summer camp that year. Today we have adopted a mission statement that reflects our current interest in education: *The Gulati Family Foundation's primary mission is to support education at every level, from early childhood through graduate school. The Foundation gives consideration to all students without discrimination. The Trustees of the Foundation believe that education ultimately provides the means for individuals to lead productive lives and contribute to society.* Rosemary manages the foundation for the family—no small task, as the Internal Revenue Service requires that meticulous records be kept to assure that the money is going to eligible organizations and that the foundation is living up to its mission as a charitable entity.

Contributions can be made in the form of cash or contributed services, of course, and so when I was asked by the President and Trustees of Chestnut Hill College to join the Board of Trustees,

I agreed. My term began in 2005. Always a believer in higher education, (despite my less-than-stellar performance in college), I have found that such service allows me to help shape the future of one of Philadelphia's oldest, small colleges. The need for major revenue at such institutions is constant, and as a result, when the institution decided to launch a new capital campaign, Rosemary and I stepped forward to serve as co-chairs.

Lessons Learned: *There are several lessons to be learned from this experience. First, it is possible to start small. One does not need to be wealthy to establish a foundation. The key is to make contributions to the foundation regularly. While there is no need to make monthly or quarterly investments, if a foundation is to grow to a size that allows for gifts of some notable sum, it must be funded whenever people have significant windfalls. Second, it is important to identify causes in which the family has demonstrated interest; that way they will be happy to see the money disbursed. Third, the foundation can be used as a legacy to children and grandchildren to teach them the importance of giving back, and inspire in them a sense of responsibility for sharing the good fortune that has come their way.*

Transitioning to Retirement

Everyone contemplates retirement at some time. It is my contention that, putting aside medical issues, both non-financial and financial issues are equally important and have to be planned and executed with the same vigor exhibited in planning one's career. Unfortunately, many people are too busy to pay significant attention to retirement planning, and when they do, they pay attention entirely to finances, with little or no attention to the non-financial issues. In today's America overall life expectancy is seventy-eight years, and thanks to better medical care, this age is expected to increase. If you were to retire today, it is very likely that you will live another twenty-five to thirty-five years, almost the same number of years you may have worked.

Retirement will be a major change in your life. During your work years, time was your scarcest resource, and you had money to spend; in retirement the reverse is true - you will have more time and less money. To retire successfully and be happy in retirement, you need to first prepare a comprehensive plan that starts by answering some basic questions such as what activities would you enjoy in your retirement, and when would be the best time to retire? How are you going to keep yourself busy? Where would you like to retire? Are there sufficient finances for your desired retirement lifestyle?

While all these questions have to be answered concurrently, you should start by determining what life style you would enjoy. Clearly, if your health permits, you will want to live an active life in your retirement years. Even though you will have more free time, no reasonable life span will allow you to do everything, so start by defining what priorities are most important to you. You may want to travel the world, become more involved with your children or grandchildren, go back to school and learn new skills, learn about the environment, go fishing often, or just play golf. You and your spouse, if you are married, are in control of the correct answers. However, you and your spouse don't have to always pursue the same interests in retirement. One spouse may be interested in travel, while the other simply wants to stay at home and play golf or go fishing. There is nothing wrong, for example, with one spouse signing up with Elderhostel for a group trip that will take him or her to a place that combines travel and education. You may decide to retire near your grandchildren, or you may live near one child for a year and then move to a location closer to another child. The choices are limitless, but you have to think them through. For me, "what" comes down to being totally relaxed and spending time boating and golfing because I had already traveled the world and had established a plan for twice-yearly trips with family. Settling how you want to spend your retirement will make it easier to answer the next questions.

Most of the time choosing "when" to retire is a personal decision; however, circumstances can force your retirement. You can experience health problems, suffer burnout, or be laid-off from a company that downsizes or closes, and the economy may offer minimal opportunities to get back into the work force. If you choose your own retirement date, you have the option to take early retirement, perhaps at age fifty-five, or you may retire at sixty-five or older. The age that you retire determines how you set up your retirement. If you retire at fifty-five, you will need a longer range plan than you will at sixty-five or older. Your investments need to last longer, and social security won't start until age sixty-two at the earliest. In addition, there are penalties and restrictions on accessing IRA and 401K retirement accounts prior to age fifty-nine and a half. Likewise, if you have a pension, you need to check what you can expect to receive throughout retirement. Another factor to keep in mind is that Medicare health insurance coverage does not start until age sixty-five, and you need to make sure you have other health insurance coverage that will provide for you and your spouse until you become eligible. Finally, you may want to consider starting a small business, a consulting business, or finding some alternative way to supplement your income. You may need to have other sources of income, at least for a few years.

When considering retirement, especially at younger ages, you need to realize that there is a work-retirement tradeoff. For each additional year you work, you should be able to generate funds adequate to cover an additional two to three years of retirement. If you do not take out any funds from your retirement nest egg, each extra year of work could add approximately 6 percent to your retirement funds because your nest egg will have earned interest, and now you will have additional funds from your salary to invest. Lastly, you can extend the age at which you begin collecting Social Security. Social Security benefits rise by roughly 8 percent a year for each year you delay taking benefits between ages sixty-two and seventy. These strategies can add 6 percent to your nest egg and 8 percent to your Social Security income for each year you continue to work.

What is the best age to start your benefits? There is no one "best age" for everyone and, ultimately, it is your choice. You should make an informed decision about when to apply for benefits based on your individual and family circumstances. Your monthly benefit amount can differ substantially based on the age when you start receiving benefits. If you decide to start benefits before full retirement age, your benefit will be smaller, but you will receive monthly income for a longer period of time. At full retirement age or later, you will receive a larger monthly benefit for a shorter period of time. However, the amount you receive when you first get benefits sets the base for the amount you will receive for the rest of your life.

Next, you need to carefully identify where you want to live in your retirement years. You may remain in your current home, purchase a year-round residence in a distant or near community, or select a seasonal home. The Mason-Dixon Poll, conducted in 2011, reports that health care, climate, low taxes, and housing are the most important factors to retirees. It is not uncommon for people to jump to conclusions about their ideal retirement location without investigating how living there will permit the lifestyle they envision. For some people, their current residence may be just perfect. In my case, the decision took multiple turns. At first I thought I would have enjoyed retiring to Myrtle Beach or Hilton Head, where we had some friends. But instead of rushing off to South Carolina, Rosemary and I decided that it was too important a decision to be made without serious thought and deliberation. During my six-month sabbatical from my businesses, I spent time investigating places that had some interest to us.

To start the process, Rosemary and I considered several criteria to evaluate the suitability of potential locations. Our criteria included easy travel to and from Philadelphia where our children and grandchildren live, availability of quality medical care, as well as the availability of sports, recreational, and cultural activities. Since we live in the northeast and winter can be brutal, we wanted a winter home in a warm climate. Of course, we wanted to live in a community that was compatible with our way of life. Income and estate taxes were also an important consideration. We first developed a short list of locales that included the Caribbean and Cayman Islands, Nevada, Baja Peninsula, Southern Florida, the Carolinas, Arizona, Switzerland, and Spain. Previously we had traveled extensively to most of these places; thus we were familiar with them. After a short discussion we ruled out foreign lands, Arizona and Nevada, mainly because of the travel distance. What remained were Southern Florida, the Carolinas, and the Cayman Islands. We traveled to these places, and, in the end, we chose Southwest Florida to be our winter home because it met all our criteria. We kept our current home in Pennsylvania for the rest of the year and our condo in New Jersey to visit for long weekends in the summer. Having narrowed down the selection to Southwest Florida, we decided to rent for awhile until we were certain that the area met our needs.

Another consideration to keep in mind as you get older is where you want to be located when you can no longer live independently, and need to move to an assisted living or nursing facility. Do you want to remain in your retirement location or relocate to where your family lives? It would not surprise me if Rosemary and I eventually head back to Pennsylvania after retiring in Florida because we would want to be near our family.

In what type of home do you want to live? Regardless of the geographical area you have selected for your retirement, you have many options for choosing what type home you want. Your retirement home should allow you to maintain your independence, that is, it should be easy to lock up and leave, and it should be accessible at all levels so you can "age in place." It may perhaps be on one floor or have access to multiple floors by an elevator that can accommodate a wheel chair, should you need one in the future. You can pay millions for a home or fifty thousand, depending on your financial capabilities and desired life style. Many retirees in Florida live in prefabricated home developments or mobile home parks. All of them enjoy the lifestyle they have outlined for themselves because they appreciate the interconnectedness of such communities where neighbors know each other and frequently participate in group activities. Making friends and getting involved in activities is not difficult because everyone is transplanted from somewhere and is looking to make new friends and get involved.

Finally, there's the question of finances. Clearly, since you do not know how long you will live, you need to be certain that you can apportion your retirement income including Social Security, any pensions, and life-long savings accordingly. Of course, you should plan your finances based on post-retirement expenses; there may be some bills you will not have to pay once you put aside your work clothes. For example, you might decide to stop paying for life insurance if you bought a policy to cover an event that has passed. You may have planned to provide your spouse money to raise the children in the event of your death; if your children have grown, this policy is no longer necessary. You may find your expenses for mortgage or entertainment will also change when you retire. Then you can determine if you have enough money to live in the way you wish. If you do not, you may have to make the hard decision to work longer, but these decisions will become clear once you compare your anticipated expenses against resources. Unfortunately, no one is going to hand you a bag full of cash when you stop working, and other than maybe a reverse mortgage on your home, no one is going to lend you money for your living expenses. Here are a few things to consider as you save and invest in retirement:

1. Adjust risk according to your age and tolerance. Hopefully by now you have been saving for your retirement over a long period of time; if not, start immediately by saving small amounts regularly - the key here is regularly. At a younger age you can take higher risks in anticipation of earning a higher return. If you make a financial mistake, you have time to recoup your losses; however, when you're retired, you can't afford to make mistakes. You should scale down your exposure to stocks. Bond funds, balanced funds, and other conservative investments can help reduce risk in your retirement investments. On the other hand, it's still okay to have some exposure to stocks—that's what keeps you ahead of inflation. If you don't have growth investments, your portfolio might not accumulate the amount of money needed each year during retirement.

2. Seek professional advice. You have worked all your life and have become an expert in your field, but you may not be an expert in financial planning. Therefore, it is important to seek professional advice from a competent third party. Retirement is a major life-cycle event, so professional planning is worth the expense.

3. Stay the course. Studies show that most after-tax gains are made by long-term investors. While it is tempting and interesting to watch daily financial indices and it is easy to be swayed by idle talk at cocktail parties, information received by these methods is not the recipe for wealth accumulation. It does not mean, however, that you should not adjust your portfolio periodically. Of the original thirty stocks that formed the Dow Jones index, only General Electric remains today. Therefore, it is critical that you review your portfolio quarterly or semi-annually and adjust your investments as your circumstances and objectives change, always keeping in mind your needs, age, and appetite for risk. Also, men and women have different tolerances for risk. Women are usually more conservative; therefore, it is necessary to find common ground that satisfies both you and your spouse. Neither one later wants to hear, "I told you so."

4. Plan for your short-term, foreseeable expenses. Clearly, as you retire, your sources of income and expenses change. Therefore, prior to your retirement, you should prepare a budget based on your soon-to-be new reality. You will need income to cover your budgeted expenses plus allowances for the unexpected. In your quarter or semi-annual review with your advisor you should plan to have sufficient funds available regardless of the fluctuations of the stock market.

Some Final Thoughts on Getting Started as an Entrepreneur

At this point I have shared my life story and highlighted some lessons that might help aspiring and practicing entrepreneurs improve their chances for success in the businesses of their choice. I have explained how I got started, what obstacles I had to overcome, and what I did that allowed me to reach my financial and personal goals by starting or acquiring and selling forty companies over the course of four decades. As the list of those companies in Appendix D makes clear, some of these companies were in the same industry—but many were not. I believe part of my success has come because I was willing to step out of my comfort zone to try new ventures. The list also shows that I began my career as an entrepreneur early, and was still acquiring and selling businesses just a year before I retired. The successful entrepreneur never stops looking for that next opportunity.

Of course, the most important step to take is the first one: launching a career as an entrepreneur. There may be some readers who are still hesitant about taking the plunge into entrepreneurship. Let me conclude with these "bullets" of advice:

- You must first decide if you have the passion to be an entrepreneur and are willing to work hard to make the necessary sacrifices to achieve success. Remember, not everyone is comfortable being an entrepreneur.

- There is no better way to learn about business than to just do it and learn from the experience. If you want to own a business, the first question you can ask yourself is, "What do I enjoy doing best?"

- Do research, make a plan, save six months' salary, and then go ahead and start your business. Establish a board of advisors or experienced mentors, people you trust to give you good advice.

- Do not worry too much about money to underwrite your efforts. There is money available through state and federal grants and business loans. Approach the Small Business Administration to help you. Don't let the economy of the country hold you back. While the economy is important as a whole, it is what happens to you that matters.

And remember: You will never know the joy that comes from being your own boss and creating a legacy for your family unless you make it happen. Get going and enjoy the ride.

Appendix A

Birth Horoscope

A birth horoscope, with accompanying astrology charts, was prepared by Pundit Shyam Sunder, an astrologer and palmist in Gujranwala, India, at the time of my birth.

The first part of the horoscope invokes the blessings of the Hindu God, Lord Ganesh. Lord Ganesh was an appropriate choice because he and the child were born during Bhadrapada, the sixth month of the Hindu calendar that starts on August 23rd and ends on September 22nd.

Some background information is helpful in understanding the gods mentioned. Hindu gods are called by various names: Lord Ganesh, known as the god who removes obstacles, is also known as Vinayak; his mother Durga is sometimes referred to as Gauri and Uma, and his father Shiva, known as the Destroyer or Transformer among the Hindu Trinity, is often called Shankar, Mahadev and Mahesh.

Lord Ganesh is depicted with the head of an elephant that is missing one tusk (referred to below as "tooth"). When he was a child, his father, Shiva, cut off his head. His mother broke down in utter grief and to soothe her, Shiva sent out his squad to fetch the head of any sleeping being that was facing the north. The squad found a sleeping elephant and brought back its severed head, which was then attached to the body of the boy. Shiva restored its life and made him the leader of his troops.

PART I

Om, I bow down in front of auspicious and respectable Lord Ganesh. I bow down in front of respectable Goddess Durga. I bow down in front of my respective gurus.

1. *Om, I bow down in front of God (Lord Ganesh) who helps to get rid of difficulties, who is also known as the supreme chief by Lord Brahma, Hindu scriptures, scholars, and others.*

2. *O thou with a single-toothed mouth, O thou the wisest, O the leader of all servants of Lord Shiva, O Vinayak, the son of Goddess Gauri, I pray and beg you to provide me all sorts of successes.*

3. *O Goddess Uma, O Gauri mother, O Shiva, O Goddess Durga, O Goddess Bhadra, O Goddess Bhagawati, O all the Lords of our family tree, O Goddess Chamunda, I pray and request you all to keep this child always secured.*

4. *On whose forehead God has written the child's destiny on the sixth day; hereby, his birth chart appears like a candle in the deep, dark night.*

Part II

In the family of Mr. Jagjit Lal, who is full of qualities and who leads gatherings, his wife by religion (lawfully-wedded) has given birth to a jewel of a son. Mr. Jagjit Lal is the son of Mr. Lal Laddharam, who is known by the name Gulati, who belongs to the Arora family tree, who is an ideal religious person, who is an avatar of our religion, who nourishes the cows and Brahmins, the respectable people of society.

The birth time of the child is as follows (based on the Hindu Calendar):

Year: *Shubba (auspicious) Calendar Year, Calendar Year 1998 of King Vikamaditya, Calendar Year 1963 of Shri Saka Shalivahana, 1941 A.D.*

Month: *The auspicious month of Bhadrapada, the sixth month of the Hindu calendar, during the fortnight of the krishna paksha that begins after the full moon.*

Date: *Auspicious Date 14*

Birthday: *Thursday*

Time: *Clock 46 & Seconds 9 at first, Clock 18 & Seconds 00 in Variyat Yoga; Clock 55 & Seconds 58 on the same day; Standard time of the day Clock 32*

& Seconds 40; Standard time of the night Clock 27 & Seconds 20; Combining both Clock 60 & Seconds 00.

With six days left in the month of Bhadrapada, when the date was the 25th of August, Clock 22 & Seconds 5 after sunrise, on the rise of Scorpio ascendant.

Now, as per Indian astrology the astrological birth name of the boy is Dipal Chandra, his zodiac sign is Cancer, master of his Zodiac sign is Moon, his birth yoni is the Cat, his servant class is demon, his nerves are extreme, and his class is Brahmin. May the birth of boy turn out to be good for all.

Prepared For: Ashok Kumarji Gulati

Birth Ascendant [Main Chart of Horoscope]

Zodiac Cycle

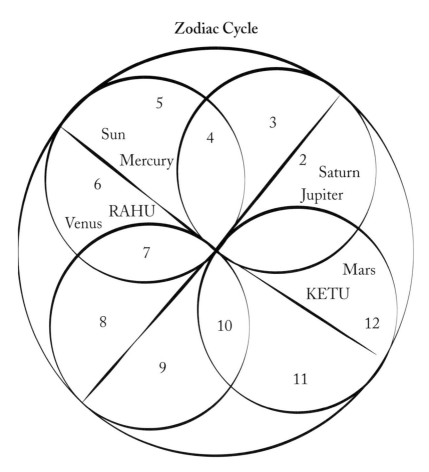

That's it! May the birth of boy turn out to be good for all.
That's it!

SS Reg. No. 1221
Pundit Shyam Sunder – Astrologer, Palmist
Gujranwala

Appendix B

Letters to My Grandchildren

Since my oldest grandchild turned twelve, I have been composing letters aimed at letting this generation know something about my life and providing them advice to help shape their futures. I have tried to combine some chatty, personal information with more weighty matters in order to hold the interest of someone his age. To give readers of this book a sample of what these letters contain, I am reproducing two of them here.

Sample letter Number 1.

April 19, 2009
Bonita Springs, Florida 34134

Dear David:
(To be distributed to other Grandchildren as they get older)

This is your Grandpa G writing. I thought that as I get older and my grandchildren come to an age at which they have a greater understanding of things, I ought to start writing them monthly letters. I will start with you, as you now have a better understanding of your worldly surroundings. As my other grandchildren come to age, I will include them in my writings as well.

So this is my first such letter. It is almost the end of the winter session, which your grandmother and I spend in our home in Florida. We had a good winter season in Florida this year. I played a lot more golf than I usually do, and I also did a lot more work than I usually do, so it is indeed a good time to come up north and enjoying the spring season. This is the time that snow should be gone, and soon the flowers will start to blossom in the north.

It would have been great to have you come to Florida during your winter breaks, but I understand it was not possible this year, due to scheduling. At age 13 you are not allowed to travel by yourself, but next winter you will be 14 and will be allowed to travel alone. Then it may be easier; perhaps you and some of your friends who are also 14 will have more flexibility and can come to visit us for a few days. We will go fly fishing and play some golf together, and in the evening we will tell each other about our life experiences. It would be fun to have you.

I am supposed to have retired, but it is not just possible to drop one's usual habits. For the last twenty-five years I have worked on the average twelve hours every weekday and have enjoyed it very much. In the past few weeks an opportunity presented itself and I purchased a restaurant called Stokesay Castle in Reading. The question that I have been asked many times is why I would take on a new project of this magnitude at my age. Well, the answer is: VISION. You see, everything starts with a vision. Vision helps you see, not what a situation is today, but what it can be in the future . . . what do you want it to be? It is like studying; your vision is to make the distinguished honor roll in your class . . . it is like playing a competitive sport; your vision is to make the team and then make a contribution to win and help your team reach the companionship game. You can just visualize winning the prize.

My vision for this property is to make it a "destination restaurant with banquet facilities," and in the next few years add a small boutique hotel and conference center. By a "destination" place I mean that, when people think of fine dining or having a reception such as wedding or school prom, they will automatically think about the wonderful place called Stokesay Castle.

In order for visions to become a reality, they require a lot of hard work. You know that in order to reach your vision of achieving distinguished honors in school you have to study hard, and that to reach the championship game you have to practice long hours—but at the same time you can have fun doing it. In fact, you have to be better than everyone else. The same applies for me; I have to make sure that I hire the best people in the restaurant business and pay attention to achieving the main objectives of my vision, taking things one step at a time. We must all realize that with any vision you seldom reach the goal in a "straight line" . . . there are often detours and setbacks . . . but one has to make corrections and try again.

David, I am also looking forward to having you make a small but important contribution to achieve my vision, when you and your friends come this summer to work at the Castle. I think it will indeed be a good experience for you to see how, taking one step at a time, a vision can become a reality. You will be proud to say that you made a contribution. But right now your vision has to be making sure you study hard as well as practice your sports; I am sure you know that they are both important to you.

Till next time . . . write if you can.

Grandpa G.

Sample letter Number 2.

June 27, 2009
Avalon N.J. 08202

Dear David;

(To be distributed to other Grandchildren as they get older)

This is your Grandpa G writing again; even though I am writing this letter in June '09, it is meant to be the May letter. You see, I was indeed looking forward to writing this letter in the latter part of May; until mid-May I had plenty of time in my hands, but it was not end of the month yet. Then all of a sudden, I got very busy and while writing this letter has been on my mind, I just did not get around to writing it. This has a plus and a minus; the minus is that you get to read this letter later than you would have, but the plus is (assuming I am on time) the June letter will also be coming soon. This reminds me of my younger years (or even now): whenever I got something good to eat, I would save the best part of it to be eaten last, in the hope I would enjoy it more—but sometimes I would forget all about it . . . oh, well.

Since my last writing Grandma G and I have returned from our house in Florida to our house in Oley. The Florida house in now closed for the summer and fall months, and we are now spending our time in Oley. On Memorial Day we opened our house in Avalon and stayed there for that weekend. Avalon had the best Memorial Day weather for a long time; normally it is raining or cold at this time of the year.

While I am little sad to be leaving Florida (you see, Florida is like an extended vacation, playing lots of golf, etc.), I always anticipate coming back from Florida at the end of April to Oley. Oley is my favorite home. I just love to wake up in the morning and see the nice grounds and trees, while I still lay in bed. It has now become a habit for me to wake up around 6:00 a.m. and stay in bed till 7:00 a.m., just enjoying the outdoor scenery and listening to the radio for news, weather and sports information. In the evening when I come home from work, as I pull up my driveway and see my big house, I visualize a peaceful place.

Opening up the Oley house is also a challenge for Grandma G. Unlike our other houses, it normally requires a lot of work. It is the biggest house we have, over 8,200 square feet; by comparison, the one in Florida is 3,200 sq. ft., and the home in Avalon is 1,650 sq. ft. In addition to the normal cleaning required because the house has been closed for four months, there is always something that needs to be fixed or replaced. This presents a challenge for Grandma G., as I am not much of a help. Even though she has a cleaning lady come to help her, there is so much to do it keep her busy for weeks on end—and in Grandma G's house, everything has to be clean and super clean. For me it is much easier, I just go to work. I work all day, which I enjoy, and come home at dinner time. Grandma G cooks a wonderful dinner most nights, except on Fridays when she and I like to go to one of our favorite local watering holes, the Pike Township Sportsman's Club, when we are on Oley and to the Avalon Yacht Club when we are in Avalon. At both places the bartenders know us, and before we even get to our seats at the bar they have Manhattans already prepared, just the way we like them. We normally have one drink at the bar, and after that we always have a nice dinner.

The other day, I was watching the golf channel; it had a special on Arnold Palmer, basically his biography. I did not get to watch the whole show, but the part I watched reminded me of you—actually, of one of your shirts, which has printed on the back the slogan, "The Harder I Work the Luckier I Get." The part that reminded me of you was when Arnold was young (a yet unproven lad, not having won his first major tournament). While he was sitting in the club house, he overheard an established player (whose name I cannot remember, but I think it was Ben Hogan) say, this lad will never win a major.

This bothered Arnold, but it also reminded him of the three keys for winning. (1) Work harder than your opponent; (2) Work smarter than your opponent; (3) Intimidate your opponent. Right then Arnold figured out that his opponent was trying to intimidate him. Arnold did not let his opponent's comment get to him. He kept his mind on the game and went on to win his first major championship. The other day Golf magazine came across my desk, and I saw similar comments expressed by Tiger Woods. I am enclosing this write-up for you to read. Maybe, if in the future you are required to do some kind of research and write an article for your studies, you may think about choosing as a topic a biography of Arnold Palmer, or key parameters of winning, or the characteristics of intimidators. Another thought that comes to my mind is the definitions of "Luck." I have always remembered ever since I was a little boy (I can't remember who said it, but I have always remembered it) that the definition of Luck is "where preparedness meets an opportunity." Clearly you have to work harder and smarter to be prepared to meet the opportunity.

I have been very busy since the second week of May to the second half of June; now it is more relaxing. I will tell you more about that in my June letter. The Stokesay Castle renovations are coming along very well. Lot of demolition has been completed. Mr. Miller, who did your pool, and Mr. Murphy (you play baseball with his son) have been working there since early May. I am still looking forward to having you and two of your friends come work with me during your summer break. Let me know when you are ready. Work is hard, pay is reasonable, but the satisfaction of seeing the Stokesay Castle vision come to realization is priceless.

Till next time . . . write if you can.

Grandpa G.

APPENDIX C

Announcing My Retirements from:
Fidelity Technologies
TeleAlarm Group
SafetyCare Technologies, Transrex AG,
Stokesay Castle, Avalon Technologies

Jack D. Gulati
Chairman and CEO
2501 Kutztown Road
Reading, PA 19605-2961
Phone: (610) 929-2444 Ext. 134
Fax: (610) 929-6861
E-mail: gulatij@fidelitygroupe.com

UNITED STATES

Fidelity Technologies Corporation
2501 Kutztown Road
Reading, PA 19605-2961
Phone: (610) 929-3330
Fax: (610) 929-6861
http://www.fidelitytech.com

Fidelity TeleAlarm, LLC
2501 Kutztown Road
Reading, PA 19605-2961
Phone: (610) 929-4200
Fax: (610) 929-6861
http://www.fidelityteleAlarm.com

Fidelity Investment Corporation
P.O. Box 563
Wayne, PA 19087-0563
Phone: (610) 989-9895
Fax: (610) 989-9985

EUROPE

Telectronic S.A.
176, rue du Nord
CH-2300 La Chaux-de-Fonds
Switzerland
Phone: + 4132 911 1111
Fax: + 4132 911 1100
http://www.telectronic.ch
http://www.telealarm.ch

Fidelity Investment Corporation
Swiss Branch
La Chaux-de-Fonds, Switzerland

JDG Holding S.A.
La Chaux-de-Fonds, Switzerland

Antenna TeleAlarm AB
Kalix, Sweden

Antenna TeleAlarm GmbH
Rodgau, Germany

Antenna Care U.K. Ltd.
Teessido, England, UK

Antenna Care BeNeLux B.V.
Gouda, The Netherlands

Antenna Care Asia Ltd.
Hong Kong, China

December 17, 2003

Dear Friends and Colleagues:

When I started Fidelity Technologies in 1988, part of my dream was to build a successful company that could continue into the next generation. With all of your help during these past years, I am proud to say that the time has come for me to realize that dream. Effective January 1, 2004 my three sons David, Charles, and Michael, will purchase the company from me. They will be the 100% outright owners of Fidelity Technologies. Furthermore, Fidelity Technologies will no longer be part of Fidelity Group.

I believe that David, Charles, and Michael have earned the right to succeed me at Fidelity Technologies. David joined the Fidelity Group ten years ago; Chuck has been with us for six years, and Michael for five years. During these years they have clearly demonstrated that they are up to this task. I would not make this decision if I did not have full confidence in their abilities to continue the tradition of excellence, and thus provide the greatest possible value to our customers, our employees, and our country. In fact, I am convinced that their enthusiasm and management skills, coupled with your assistance, will move the Fidelity Technologies colleagues that you show them the same level of commitment that you have always given to me.

I will now concentrate on the healthcare companies: Avalon Technologies, TeleAlarm, and Antenna, with the expectation that putting my full energies into these endeavors will yeild great success. As part of this, TeleAlarm Worldwide (including both Anten-

270

na and TeleAlarm US) and Avalon Technologies LLC will continue to report to Pierre-Alain Nicati and Chris Ross, respectively. They will report directly to me. During the first quarter of next year, I will move my office out of Reading to a yet undetermined location.

I have always believed that there are several stages in life, and now is my time to refine my focus and pursue new ventures and activities. You all know that I have great passion for the work we are doing in the healthcare arena and the potential it has to improve the quality of life of the world's seniors. I am certain that with your help, we can continue to build another great group of companies.

I have great confidence in the leadership that Pierre-Alain and Chris will provide for the companies and I will do everything I can assist them in their drive for excellence and success. I ask for your support as we all undertake these endeavors.

My warmest regards,

September 30, 2006   CONFIDENTIAL TILL MONDAY,
                           OCTOBER 2, 2006 10:00 AM

Dear Colleagues and Friends;

Today I am announcing that I have sold TeleAlarm Group – Europe to Bosch Security Systems of Ottobrunn, Germany. This is another step in the ongoing consolidation of our industry.

I regret that I cannot be with all of you in person to make this announcement. I can assure you that this was not an easy decision for me, nor was it made lightly. These have been very emotional times for me as I have, over the years, come to love this company, and I have enjoyed going to work each and every day with vigor and enthusiasm. Regardless of the challenges that I faced, I always thought of each challenge as an opportunity to make our Group better.

During these years, we have had our ups and downs, but, overall, thanks to your dedication and high spirits, I think we have made good progress. As most of you know, our industry has changed considerably over the last two years. Clearly the "care for the elderly" market has grown and will continue to grow significantly. Industry consolidation has created an environment where companies require significant resources to compete effectively.

When I first bought Telectronic SA thirteen years ago, many companies competed, but basically their business was concentrated in their home country, just as we were in Switzerland. It was a time conducive to entrepreneurship. However, today's business environment requires that companies compete on a European-wide basis, if not a world-wide basis. The marketplace today does not provide just Carephones; customers seek total solutions the "Care of the Elderly at Home". Over the years TeleAlarm has clearly met the challenges by expanding its product lines and geographical marketplace, both organically and through acquisition. The company now requires significant infusion of capital to continue to be an innovative leader in the industry and to further extend its geographic and products reach.

This year we at TeleAlarm celebrated our 50th year anniversary. It is my deep desire to see that TeleAlarm meets the challenges it will face for the next fifty years. About a year ago I started to think how TeleAlarm Group could best meet the challenges of the future. My main objective was to create an environment where TeleAlarm can meet these challenges with greater certainty.

After much thought, a fair amount of consultation and considering all options, I have come to the conclusion that TeleAlarm Group will be in the best of hands with Bosch. I have known Bosch's top management for over ten years with very high regards. I know their management style and their passion for this industry. I believe they have the resources and desire to be the "best in class," and I believe they will succeed.

I would be very much appreciative if you give Bosch the same dedication you have always given me. While from now on we will not be business colleagues, please remember that you are also my friends. This sale should not prohibit us from being friends. I intend to maintain good contact with you all, and I hope you will consider the same.

I am indeed thankful to you all for your service to this company. I wish you all the best of everything in the future.

Best regards,
Jack Gulati

Avalon Technologies LLC
SafetyCare Technologies LLC
Stokesay Castle LLC
Stokesay Real Estate LLC
Transrex AG

August 29, 2011

Dear Friends and Colleagues:

In 2009, I returned from a three-year retirement to become engaged in the business world again, as I felt that I still had energy left in me to continue to work and create business activities which will have lasting effects.

During this time I took over the management of Avalon Technologies and created SafetyCare Technologies and Stokesay Castle. In January 2010, I purchased Transrex and Synapse located in Switzerland (thereafter merged together and known as Transrex). These have been challenging times, and I must say I have enjoyed working with my wonderful and talented colleagues both here and abroad. My special thanks to you all for making my work enjoyable. I have always looked forward to every day.

However, during the recent past, I have noticed, that the challenges presented in managing these entities into their next level of achievements are beyond my capabilities and energy. Thus in discussions with my wife, Rosemary, my sons David, Charles, and Michael and many of you, I have decided to once again retire from my business activities. I will turn 70 next year, so the timing is correct . . . Let the next level of management be younger and more talented than I.

I am very fortunate to have three very talented and business "battle proven" sons, who have agreed to acquire all of these companies from me. Therefore, effective immediately Chuck, who is currently General Manager of Military and Aerospace division at Fidelity Technologies, will take over the management of all of companies mentioned above. He will be assisted by Michael, who will, in addition to his responsibilities at Fidelity, become CFO of these companies as well. I will be around until December 31, 2011, in an advisory and transition role, to provide any assistance that Chuck or anyone of you may need. Effective January 1, 2012, it is anticipated that David, Charles and Michael will acquire the ownership of all these companies from me.

I believe that David, Charles and Michael have earned the right to own and manage these companies. In 2004 I sold Fidelity Technologies to them. In the years following they have grown Fidelity at a 25 percent compounded rate, year after year. This is indeed quite an achievement, especially when one considers the economic times during this period. Chuck and Michael have played a significant role in achieving these results at Fidelity. I would not have taken this decision if I did not have full confidence in their abilities to continue to move these companies to the next level of growth, thus providing greatest possible value to our customers, our employees and our country. In fact, I am convinced that their enthusiasm and management skills, coupled with your assistance, will move these companies forward at a faster pace. However, they will need the support of every single one of you, and I ask all of my colleagues that you show them the same level of commitment that you have always given me.

I thank you all for your support and dedication to these companies and for being my friends.

My warmest regards,
Jack Gulati

Appendix C

Companies Owned

Name	Year Started	Year Bought	Year Disposed	Years Owned	Business Description	Disposition	Age at Start of Business	Age at Time of Disposal
El-Tech Manufacturing Company Inc.		1968	1972	4	Electronic contract manufacture	Closed	26	30
Medical Computer Services Inc.	1971		1972	1	Billing & collections for Physicians' offices	Closed due to pending divorce	29	30
Entry Equipment Limited	1972		1973	1	Facility Entry equipment distributor	Sold back to the Partners	30	31
Market Study Associates		1972	1973	1	Preformed market studies in the computer industry	Sold back to the Partner	30	31
Diva Inc.		1973	1975	2	Electronic contract manufacture	Closed	31	33
Triester International Investments	1973		1974	1	International money management firm [I had an independent agency within this company]	Closed	31	32
Community Computer Corporation		1974	1980	6	Provided time-share computer services	Sold back to the Partners	32	38

General Automotive Products Inc.	1974		1976	2	Designed and manufactured Remote Control Automobile Starters	Sold to Pennfield	32	34
FIC Associates I (Limited Partnership)	1977		1985	8	Builders Model Home & Lease Back Program	Company liquidated–all assets sold	35	43
Fidelity Investment Corporation	1977		2012	35	Real estate Investments; shell company used to purchase other companies; acted as General Partner in Limited Prtnerships	Still active	35	70
FIC Associates XIX (Limited Partnership)	1980		2002	22	Airport Real Estate Investment	Company liquidated–all assets sold	38	60
Viatek Inc.		1984	1987	3	Designed and manufactured wireless products	Majority Partner Takeover	42	45
Bensalem Auto Body Shop (Partnership)		1985	1987	2	Reconditioned automobiles for resale	Partnership dissolved	43	45
Fidelity Technologies Corporation	1987		2004	17	Defense contracting	Sold to my sons	45	62

Name	Year Started	Year Bought	Year Disposed	Years Owned	Business Description	Disposition	Age at Start of Business	Age at Time of Disposal
Cossonay Metrology Systems Corporation	1992		1998	6	Distributor & service provider of Metrology systems	Merged into Fidelity Technologies Corp	50	56
Cossonay Metrology Systems SA	1992		1995	3	Designed & manufactured Metrology systems	Merged into Fidelity Technologies Corp	50	53
FDL Technologies Corporation		1992	1994	2	Government contractor	Merged into Fidelity Technologies Corp	50	52
Gulati & Company	1992		1998		Holding Company	Dissolved	50	56
Telectronic SA - TeleAlarm SA (name Change)	1993		2004	11	Designed and manufactured of Medical Emergency Alert systems & wireless nurse call systems	Merged into TeleAlarm Group Holding SA	51	62

Company				Description	Status		
Telectronic Corporation – Fidelity TeleAlarm LLC – TeleAlarm LLC (Name Changes)	1994	2011	17	Distributor & service provider of Medical Emergency Alert systems & wireless nurse call systems in USA	Merged into SafetyCare Technologies LLC	52	69
Telectronic GmbH	1994	2001		Distubutor & service provider of Medical Emergency Alert systems & wireless nurse call systems in Germany	Merged into TeleAlarm GmbH	52	59
Fidelity Investment Corporation Swiss Branch	1995	2012	17	Owner of an industrial building (Telectronic) in Switzerland	Company liquidated-all assets sold	53	70
General Data Systems Ltd.	1976	1981	5	Data Processing software developer	Sold back to the Partners	34	39
JDG Holding SA	1997	2002	1	Holding Company	Dissolved	55	60
Antenna AB	2001	2001	1	Holding Company	Dissolved	59	59
Antenna Care AB - TeleAlarm Nordic AB (Name Change)	2001	2004	3	Designed and manufactured Emergency Response Systems	Merged into TeleAlarm Group Holding SA	59	62
Antenna Care Asia Ltd.	2001	2002	1	Distributor & service provider of Emergency Response Systems in China	Closed	59	60

Name	Year Started	Year Bought	Year Disposed	Years Owned	Business Description	Disposition	Age at Start of Business	Age at Time of Disposal
Antenna Care BeNeLux – TeleAlarm BV (Name Change)		2001	2004	3	Distributor & service provider of Emergency Response Systems in Netherlands & Belgium	Merged into TeleAlarm Group Holding SA	59	62
Antenna Care GmbH		2001	2002	1	Distributor & service provider of Emergency Response Systems in Germany	Merged into TeleAlarm GmbH	59	60
Antenna Care UK Ltd. – TeleAlarm Ltd. (Name Change)		2001	2004	3	Distributor & service provider of Emergency Response Systems in United Kingdom	Merged into TeleAlarm Group Holding SA	59	62
Antenna Development AB		2001	2001	1	Developed and constructed technically advanced radio and communications products and systems	Sold to Microbit	59	59

Company					Description	Status		
TeleAlarm GmbH	2001		2006	5	Distubutor & service provider of Medical Emergency Alert systems & wireless nurse call systems in Germany	sold to Bosch	59	64
Avalon Technologies LLC		2002	2011	9	Designed and manufactured communication systems for assisted living facilities	Merged into SafetyCare Technologies LLC	60	69
Asset Management Advisors	2004		2012	8	Insurance Sales	Still active	62	70
TeleAlarm Group Holding SA	2004		2006	2	Holding Company	sold to Bosch	62	64
SafetyCare Technologies LLC	2008		2011	3	Monitoring Center for medical emergency alarms	Gifted to Sons	66	69
Stokesay Castle LLC	2009		2011	2	Restaurant & banquet facility	Gifted to Sons	67	69
Stokesay Real Estate LLC	2009		2011	2	Real estate Investments	Gifted to Sons	67	69

Name	Year Started	Year Bought	Year Disposed	Years Owned	Business Description	Disposition	Age at Start of Business	Age at Time of Disposal
Synapse SA	2010		2011	1	Designed and manufactured watch transmitters for emergency alert systems	Merged into Transrex AG	68	69
Transrex AB	2010		2011	2	Designed and manufactured patient communications systems for Hospitals	Gifted to Sons	68	69

A Note on Sources

The following works were consulted in order to provide background for my personal story:

For information in the Introduction: Robert Kiyosaki, *Rich Dad's Retire Young, Retire Rich* (2002); Douglas Brinkley, *Wheels for the World: Henry Ford, His Company, and a Century of Progress, 1903-2003* (2003).

For information on India's history: H. A. Rose, Denzil Ibbetson, and Edward Maclagan, *A Glossary of the Tribes and Castes of the Punjab and North-West Frontier Province* (1911); Lakshmi Chandra Jain, *Indigenous Banking In India* (1929); "Gandhi Joins the Immortals," *Life* (1948); Khushwant Singh, *Train to Pakistan* (1956); Allen Hayes Merriam, *Gandhi vs. Jinnah: The Debate over the Partition of India* (1980); Trevor Royle, *The Last Days of the Raj* (1997); Stanley Wolpert, *Shameful Flight: The Last Years of the British Empire in India* (2006); Ian J. Kerr,

Engines of Change: The Railroads That Made India (2007); Robyn Meredith, *The Elephant and the Dragon: The Rise of India and China and What It Means for All of Us* (2008).

For information on New York in the 1950's, 1960's, and 1970's: Alphonso Pinkney and Roger R. Woock, *Poverty and Politics in Harlem* (1970); Francois Weil, *A History of New York,* translated by Jody Gladding (2004); George J. Lankevich, *American Metropolis: A History of New York City* (1998).

For information relating to my first marriage and divorce: Glenna Spitze and Scott South, "Women's Employment, Time Expenditure and Divorce," *Journal of Family Issues* (September 1985); C. L. Strow and B. K. Strow, "A History of Divorce and Remarriage in the United States," *Humanomics* (2006); Eric W. Doherty and William J. Doherty, "Smoke Gets in Your Eyes: Cigarette Smoking and Divorce in a National Sample of American Adults," *Family Systems and Health* (Winter 1998); "A study of recent trends shows that divorce cases are significantly rising in small towns and semi-urban areas," *Tribune On-Line Edition,* 17 July 2007; "Smoking May Raise Breast Cancer Risk," *Health.com* (24 January 2011).

For information on Fidelity Investment Corporation, including inflation and mortgage rates in the 1970's and 1980s, and my investment history and philosophy: Stephen Koepp and Thomas McCarron, "Maryland: Time Bomb Goes Off," *Time* (27 May 1985); Edward Nelson, "The Great Inflation of the Seventies: What Really Happened?" Federal Reserve Bank of St. Louis Working Paper Series: Working Paper 2004-001 (January 2004); "The Roots of the Mortgage Crisis: The 1970's" (www.

foreclosurefish.net/foreclosureblog/2008/09/-the-roots-of-the-mortgage-crisis).

For information on United Chem-Con and my efforts to buy assets to form Fidelity Technologies: "A Hi-Tech Moneymaker," *Black Enterprise* (February 1983); "New Group on the Block" (June 1986); Ron Devlin, "Renovo is a Passenger on an Economic Roller Coaster," *Allentown Morning Call* (18 December 1988); "Three Get Jail Terms in Defense Contract Fraud," *Allentown Morning Call* (25 February 1989); "Chem-Con Official Sentenced for Defense Contract Fraud," *Allentown Morning Call* (22 April 1989); Dick Cowen, "Chem-Con President Gets Six Years, Fine, Probation," *Allentown Morning Call* (9 June 1989); "British Firm Claims it was Duped," *Washington Post* (29 September 1989); James Traub, *Too Good to be True: The Outlandish Story of WedTech* (1990); "Congressman Charged with Taking Bribes," *Associated Press* (6 May 1992).

For information on growth at Fidelity Technologies: Roberta Maynard, "University Ties Give Companies an Edge," *Nation's Business* (1995); "Fidelity Saluted as Highest-Performing Company in Greater Reading," *Made in PA Magazine* (2010); Rebecca Vandermuelen; "Portable Generators Power Defense Contractor's Rapid Growth," *Eastern Pennsylvania Business Journal* (2010); "No. 1: Fidelity Technologies Corp.," *Reading Eagle* (9 May 2010); David Gulati, "Lean Principles are More than Words," *Manufacturing Business Technology* (www/mbtmag. com/content.aspx?id=1427).

For information on my other business ventures, including Viatek, TeleAlarm, SafetyCare and Avalon Technologies: Tom Moylan,

"State Commerce Secretary Says Lehigh Valley On 'Cutting Edge' of High-Tech Industry Growth," *Allentown Morning Call* (19 September 1985); "Comdial and Fidelity TeleAlarm Sign Agreement for Avalon Healthcare Solution," *Business Wire* (5 November 2001); "SafetyCare and TeleAlarm Form Strategic Alliance," *Security, Distributing & Marketing Magazine* (1 October 2005); "Bosch Acquires TeleAlarm Group," Bosch Group Press Release (3 October 2006); "TeleAlarm, LLC Adds New Layer of Protection by Acquiring SafetyCare," SafetyCare Press Release (11 April 2007); "SafetyCare to Unveil Emergency Response Center to Offer Enhanced Safety and Security Services," SafetyCare Press Release (19 September 2007); Tony Lucia, "Selling Peace of Mind in Muhlenberg," *Reading Eagle* (23 March 2011).

For information on Stokesay Castle: Tony Lucia, "Stokesay Castle to go to auction in March," *Reading Eagle* (26 February 2009); "Stokesay is Sold for $623,850," *Reading Eagle* (31 March 2009; David A. Kostival, "Reading Area Stokesay Castle Undergoing Renovation," *Reading Eagle* (24 August 2009); Valdis I. Lacis, "Stokesay Owner Wants to Add 66-Room Boutique Hotel," *Reading Eagle* (22 December 2009); Terry Scott Reed, "Stokesay: How Jack Gulati Saved our Castle," *Berks Business2Business* (2010).

For information on my political career and involvement with professional associations: Robert D. Lystad, "Small Business Confab Tackles Liability Insurance," *Allentown Morning Call* (22 August 1986); "Dozens Run for Spots at Party Conventions Campaign 88," *Allentown Morning Call* (1 March 1988); Anthony R. Wood, "In Upper Merion, Just the Same Old

Grind," *Philadelphia Inquirer* (24 March 1993); Joe McDermott, "GOP Bastion Has Become Wacky Scene," *Allentown Morning Call* (26 January 1994); Russell E. Eshleman, "Independent Business Alliance Endorses Ridge," *Philadelphia Inquirer* (21 January 1998); Kathy O'Loughlin, "ML History: Our Nearby Montco Townships: Upper Merion and Cheltenham," www.mainlinemedianews.com (4 August 2010).

For information on family business matters: Aron Pervin, "How Shared Leadership Can Work," *The Globe and Mail* (13 May 1999); Ivan Lensberg, *Succeeding Generations: Realizing the Dream of Family Business* (1999); John L. Ward, *Perpetuating the Family Business: 50 Lessons Learned from Long-Lasting, Successful Families in Business* (2004); Mike Henning, "Partners at the Top: Co-Leadership Arrangements can work well—but the sibling or cousin partners must be willing to establish covenants with one another based on mutual trust," *Family Business* (Summer 2008); Dennis T. Jaffe, "Making the Right Choice for a Family Successor: The decision can be consultative and collaborative without being democratic," *Family Business* (Summer 2008); "Start Giving It Away Early," *Smart Money* (25 January 2011); Kavil Ramachadandran, "The Challenge of Leadership Succession in Family Business" *Economic Times* online (17 July 2011).